The Poverty Question

The Poverty Question

Search for Solutions

Yogesh Atal

RAWAT PUBLICATIONS
Jaipur and New Delhi

ISBN 81-7033-718-6

Published by
Prem Rawat for ***Rawat Publications***
Satyam Apts., Sector 3, Jain Temple Road, Jawahar Nagar, Jaipur - 4 (India)
Phone: 0141 651748 / 657006 Fax: 0141 651748
e-mail : info@rawatbooks.com
Website: rawatbooks.com

Delhi Office
G-4, 4832/24, Ansari Road, Daryaganj, New Delhi 110 002
Phone: 011-3263290

Typeset by Rawat Computers, Jaipur
Printed at Chaman Enterprises, New Delhi

Contents

Contents

Preface

The question of poverty has come to the centre stage with the World Summit for Social Development (WSSD), held in March 1995 in Copenhagen, Denmark, expressing its commitment to eradicate it. The World Summit brought at one place around 14,000 participants that included government delegates from as many as 186 countries, and representatives of nearly 800 NGOs from all over the world. The *Copenhagen Declaration and Programme of Action* calls for an integrated approach to poverty eradication, sustainable livelihoods and social integration. It recognises the complexity of the poverty question and invites rethinking of social policies and strategies hitherto employed to combat poverty. Following the Summit, the United Nations observed the year 1996 as the International Year for the Eradication of Poverty (IYEP). The United Nations General Assembly, in its resolution 50/107 of 20 December 1995, also declared to observe the *First United Nations Decade for the Eradication of Poverty (1997-2006).*

Serving as UNESCO's Coordinator for the World Summit for Social Development I was involved in the preparatory work related to the Summit, as well as in the follow-up to the Summit. This assignment gave me an opportunity to focus on poverty-related questions, and also to encourage fellow social scientists to engage in research and reflection on this moot issue. I had the privilege of working closely with the Comparative Research Programme on Poverty (CROP) of the International Social Science Council. Through UNESCO's support, CROP came out with a publication, based on papers presented at an international conference, titled *Poverty: A Global Review* to serve as a Handbook on International Poverty Research. This was edited by Else Øyen, S.M. Miller and Syed Abdus Samad and published in 1996 jointly by UNESCO and the Scandinavian University Press.

In collaboration with CROP chairperson, Else Øyen, I organised a Round Table in Copenhagen, during the Summit on Poverty and Participation in Civil Society. The proceedings of this Round Table have also been published under our joint editorship (UNESCO and Abhinav Publications, 1997). I also edited a book for the Indian Institute of Education, Pune on *Perspectives on Educating the Poor* (Abhinav Publications, 1997). In addition, I took the initiative of commissioning six country studies on poverty in the countries of the former Soviet bloc that are now designated as "Economies in Transition". The countries covered were: Hungary, Bulgaria, Romania, Georgia, Russia, and Mongolia. Supervising these studies and editing them was a great learning experience for me. I submitted the manuscript to UNESCO as my parting gift, after having served the Organization for more than two decades. That book, the first from among the agencies within the United Nations system on poverty in Eastern Europe and as a follow-up to the WSSD, came out in 1999 under the title *Poverty in Transition and Transition in Poverty*, again as a joint publication of UNESCO and Berghahn Books, New York. All these four publications, with which I have been associated, are part of the follow-up to the WSSD and contributions to the United Nations Decade for the Eradication of Poverty. In each of the last three books, published under my editorship, I have written long "Introductions" that go beyond ritually summarising the various contributions. Using the papers and studies I have raised several questions that need to be carefully considered and systematically researched in a cross-cultural comparative framework. Taken together, they sum up my approach to the question of poverty and my views in regard to the role of education and of the civil society in poverty eradication. The essay on poverty in the countries of the former Soviet bloc adds yet another dimension to the poverty question as the situation in them is very different where the available diagnoses and prescriptions suggested for poverty eradication in the developing countries do not apply.

This collection of my essays on poverty that includes, besides the three "Introductions" mentioned above, two of my earlier essays on poverty published in early `seventies is an offering to the United Nations Decade for the Eradication of Poverty. Written at different times and in different contexts, the essays may not provide the kind of organic unity that is expected in a book, but these deserve to be read for the kind of questions they raise and the challenges they spell out for the social scientists. The reader will get at one place my contributions to the poverty debate.

I am resisting the temptation of editing them and crave the indulgence of the discerning reader to overlook inevitable "repetitions" of ideas or facts. But retaining their originality has the advantage that any essay can be read singly without reference to the other. Of course, the new "Introduction" for this book should fill the gaps or build a bridge between different essays. At the end of the book, as an annexure, the chapter on Eradication of Poverty from the Programme of Action recommended by the WSSD has been reproduced; the reader will find it a useful reference.

I sincerely hope that these essays will provoke the reader. I do not expect everyone to agree with what I say, and would welcome any serious disagreement or dialogue. The essays do not offer any ready-made prescriptions for the eradication of poverty; they constitute my search for solutions and invite others to join this journey.

Poverty still needs to be researched if we seriously wish to move from pious platitudes and administration of untested prescriptions. While the problem of poverty is global, its solutions will have to be local. We can, of course, gain insights from the experience of others, but cannot replicate their strategies. We have to bring back local culture in our scheme of things. This is the essence of the new demand for "think globally, act locally". For social sciences this is a major challenge. Let us face it.

I would like to express my thanks to Mr Kailash Rawat of the Rawat Publications for proposing to bring out this collection of my essays. I also appreciate the efficient and prompt handling of the publication.

Yogesh Atal

1

Introduction: Rethinking Poverty Issues

For more than five decades the world has focused on development and yet the destination is not in sight. The prime focus of developmental work in the past was on the eradication of poverty. And yet it is poverty that has defied all prescriptions. To be sure, radical reforms in the economy and the polity have brought about significant changes in the societies of the developing world but the ugly face of poverty still refuses to disappear. Several activities favouring the poor and against poverty were, and are being, carried out both by individual governments and the international community and yet we have sizeable number of the poor and horrifying manifestations of poverty. The Secretary-General of the United Nations admitted in his 1994 Report: "Absolute poverty, hunger, disease, and illiteracy are the lot of the one-fifth of the world's population. There can be no more urgent task for development than to attack both the causes and the symptoms of these ills. It is a task that requires action and commitment. It is an agenda that requires the widest possible distribution of development efforts, the implementation of broad-based strategies and the orientation of development efforts towards projects that enhance people rather than national prestige" (Boutros-Ghali, 1995: 38).

Recognising its dreadful implications hampering development, poverty has received critical attention in the freshly defined *Agenda for Development* under the aegis of the United Nations. In its Resolution 48/183 of 21 December 1993, the General Assembly of the United Nations proclaimed 1996 as the International Year for the Eradication of Poverty and decided to dedicate the entire decade, beginning 1997, to this task. Combating poverty is a mammoth task, and it requires careful consideration of its nature and magnitude for the proper formulation of strategies to eradicate it.

The theme of *social development*, which focuses primarily on poverty eradication, came to the centre stage in the last decades of the previous century. At that time, there was a worldwide interest in looking back at our achievements and failures, and looking forward to the kind of world we would be moving in, or the kind of world we would like to fashion for our coming generations. The United Nations, which was to complete its half century of existence in the last decade of the previous century, took the initiative in organising a series of conferences on specific themes to evaluate the past performance and to chart out a path for the future. Those conferences were not merely exercises in preparing the balance-sheet of our past gains and failures; they constructively engaged in shaping our common destiny.

A total of seven such conferences were organised by the United Nations in the 1990s. These were: The World Summit for Children (New York, September 1990), UN Conference on Environment and Development (Rio de Janeiro, June 1992), World Conference on Human Rights (Vienna, June 1993), International Conference on Population and Development (Cairo, September 1994), Fourth World Conference on Women

(Beijing, September 1995), and the United Nations Conference on Human Settlements---Habitat-II (Istanbul, June 1996). The World Summit for Social Development was the fifth in this series of seven landmark world conferences. Though held before the other two conferences on Women and on Habitat, the World Summit for Social Development was a culmination of this exercise and it anticipated the outcome of the latter two conferences and included recommendations relative to those concerns as well, utilising the results of the preparatory committee meetings organised for those events.

The UN General Assembly felt that the time had come to convene a World Summit for Social Development (WSSD) as favourable environment for social progress had been created by several developments. Through its Resolution 47/92 of 16 December 1992, the General Assembly decided to convene the Summit in March 1995, accepting the offer of Denmark to host it in Copenhagen. The decision of the General Assembly was a reaffirmation of the need for the international community to address urgent social problems of unprecedented gravity and complexity. The end of global ideological confrontation and the cold war, the spread of democratic forms of government in various parts of the world, greater openness amongst nations to tolerance and pluralism, scientific and technological innovations, and revolution in communication and information had created conditions for discussing issues related to social development. In deciding for the agenda for the Summit, the General Assembly identified three interrelated objectives, namely, alleviation and reduction of poverty, expansion of productive employment and enhancement of social integration. Focusing on the three core concerns, the World Summit emphasised the need for renewed efforts by the international community towards higher living standards, greater equality of opportunity and security of human rights.

The conferences preceding WSSD acknowledged the fact that the past five decades of development did not succeed in improving the overall development profile of the countries of the world. Of course, on all indicators of development, there were encouraging ratings: expanding rates of literacy, increasing industrialisation, rise in life expectancy, economic development, faster means of transportation and revolutionary changes in the fields of communication and information. But these achievements were not a cause for complacency. Fast depletion of resources and alarming pollution of the environment caused by mundane pursuit of economic growth questioned the very sustainability of development. The ever-widening gap between the rich and the poor resulting in exclusion and marginalisation of groups, vulgar expressions of intolerance and hatred resulting in loss of innocent lives, emergence of newer and more dangerous diseases, abuse of drugs, heinous violation of human rights and persistent illiteracy among 900 million people worldwide reminded that in our enthusiasm for rapid economic development we grossly neglected human and cultural dimensions of development. The UNDP Human Development Report for 1994 characterised the situation of the time thus: "an arresting picture of unprecedented human progress and unspeakable human misery, of humanity' s advance on several fronts mixed with humanity's retreat on several others, of a breathtaking globalisation of prosperity side by side with a depressing globalisation of poverty." The World Summit was regarded as a "call for humanity to restore its perspective and redesign its agenda".

The World Summit admitted that there was considerable unfinished agenda that required fresh prioritisation. Concern was shown to the fact that despite all the development efforts poverty was widespread with nearly 1.3 billion people suffering from severe deprivation, and many children dying every day from malnutrition in the underdeveloped regions of the world.

Underemployment still characterised the economy of most of the developing countries. Even in industrialising countries unemployment rates were reaching alarming levels. Disadvantaged groups continue to be marginalised in economic, social and political processes. Violence, intolerance, and tensions and conflicts within and among communities and nations have become all too frequent. Safeguarding the environment and achievement of sustainable development are still among the challenges confronting the international community. Above all, it was poverty that became the major concern, not only because of the sheer size of the absolute poor but because of the fact that all the countries—both developed and developing—admitted the existence of poverty. What is more is that the gap between the rich and the poor countries has also widened so that not only there are the rich and the poor families within a country but also rich and the poor nations in the world community.

The poverty question is much more complicated requiring different strategies to handle the poverty of the nations and poverty of the peoples. The rising index of a country's GDP does not automatically translate into the decline in the size of the poor of that country; similarly, the poor of a developed country may be in a much better position, relatively speaking, than the poor of a poor country. That has been one of the reasons for the United Nations Development Programme (UNDP) to restrict their statistics about the poor to the non-industrialised countries while developing the Human Poverty Index. However, to the extent the wealth of a country influences the programmes relative to poverty eradication, it is useful to know the existing gaps between the rich and the poor countries. For example, in the high-income countries that number 33 (and add to that Hong Kong) the annual per capita income is as high as US $26,000. Compare this with the annual per capita income of the absolute poor numbering nearly 1.3 billion, which is around US $393 (PPP). The richest countries constitute 14.9 per cent of the world population but have 78.4 per cent of the world's GDP, compared to 46 per cent of the poorest sharing only 1.25 per cent of the world GDP, and 39.1 per cent of the middle range countries accounting for the 20.35 per cent of the GDP share. It is also interesting to note that between 1987 and 1994 military spending worldwide declined by 3.6 per cent yielding a cumulative dividend (aptly called *peace dividend*) of US $935 billion ($810 billion among the developed countries, and $125 billion among the developing countries). But all this did not go to social spending, to promote the cause of social development. That was the reason that the UNDP and some other agencies within the United Nations system proposed a 20:20 formula suggesting that 20 per cent of all Overseas Developmental Aid (ODA) be spent on social development with a matching 20 per cent of national GDP for this purpose. It may also be noted that all the rich countries did not comply with the commitment to contribute to ODA a small sum of 0.7 per cent of GDP.

The Earth Summit, which was held in Rio de Janeiro, emphasised the need for *sustainable development*—a coinage given by the Brundtland Commission in its Report, Our Common Future—drawing attention to the deterioration of the environment and depletion of the resources. The Social Summit called for *Sustainable Human Development.* The journey from Rio to Copenhagen was, thus, a journey from ecology to sociology. Emphasising this point, Federico Mayor—the Director-General of UNESCO—said in his address to the Social Summit:

> Poverty, unemployment, social exclusion and marginalization are problems that infest all our societies—not only those of the South. Both North and South are in search of new solutions, as the old recipes and past policies have failed to address these problems. It is not only the South that needs development; the challenge is global. We can no longer allow economics to dictate our social realities. New paradigms of development are

emerging. Rio and Cairo highlighted *ecological* and *demographic* parameters of development. Copenhagen and Beijing call for consideration of the *cultural* and *social.* The message is loud and clear: economic growth should sub serve the cause of social development. It certainly should not cause social crises. The time has come to realize that while we face common problems, we may not always have common answers. We have entered an era of uncommon opportunities and we must not let them pass.

Hidden in his statement was the message that it would be wrong to pursue simplistic solutions to complex problems. Economic development alone is not enough. *Wealth* is not the answer for all our *illth.* The UNDP also acknowledged, for the first time, in its 1994 HRD Report that development in the past heavily relied on economics, and that is partially responsible for the present crisis in the social sphere. It said:

> Only during the 20th century did the social sciences become increasingly concerned with economics—and economics with wealth rather than with people, with the economy rather than with society, with maximisation of income rather than with the expansion of opportunities for people. Although the obsession with materialism may be recent, the preoccupation of economists and policy makers with augmenting "national treasure", with surplus trade balances, dates back at least to the mercantilists, who preferred to concentrate on material success rather than on the development of human lives.
>
> The dominant contemporary tradition of focusing exclusively on such variables as per capita Gross National Product or national wealth is a continuation—certainly intensification—of the old opulence-oriented approach. And it is this low road of regarding humanity as an instrument of production—rather than the high road of acknowledging the universality of life claims—that fits well with the reputation of economics as a "dismal science".

The fact that the World Summit was called a Summit for *Social* Development emphasised the concern over deficits in regard to social development. It was also a statement to the effect that economic development is not enough to ensure social development. How do we otherwise explain the existence of social crises in both the developed and the developing societies? Earlier conferences were like assemblies of the donor and the recipient countries. But the WSSD had participants who all acknowledged the crisis of social development whether they belonged to the developed First World, the Third World comprising of the countries of the South, or the countries-in-transition, i.e., the former communist world. Poverty, unemployment and socially disintegrative tendencies are the problems that trouble all the countries. All countries are deeply concerned in finding new strategies to address the problems of social development back home. No one had the answer, and they were not looking for a "cure-for-all" panacea. It was realisation of the point that economic growth alone could not solve these problems. As the UNDP Report on Human Resource Development (1994) argued, "accumulating wealth is not necessary for the fulfilment of some important human choices" and that "human choices extend far beyond economic well-being". To quote HRD Report of 1994:

> A society does not have to be rich to be able to afford democracy. A family does not have to be wealthy to respect the rights of each member. A nation does not have to be affluent to treat women and men equally. Valuable social and cultural traditions can be---and are---maintained at all levels of income. A richness of a culture can be largely independent of the people's wealth....
>
> Human beings may want to be wealthy. But they may also want to enjoy long and healthy lives, drink deep at the fountain of knowledge, participate freely in the life of their community,

> breathe fresh air and enjoy the simple pleasures of life in a clean physical environment and value the peace of mind that comes from security in their homes, in their jobs and in their society....
>
> National wealth might expand people's choices. But it might not. The use that nations make of their wealth, not the wealth itself, is decisive. And unless societies recognise that their real wealth is their people, an excessive obsession with the creation of material wealth can obscure the ultimate objective of enriching human lives (p.15).

Coming from the UNDP this was a very welcome shift in the paradigm, as it heralded a new era for the social sciences, which had suffered relative neglect all these years of economistic hegemony. To be sure, this was not to deny the importance of economic development or the role of wealth. As the UNDP itself notes: this "should not be interpreted to mean that economic growth does not matter in improving the quality of life. Instead, it indicates that the connections are seriously contingent. Much depends on how the fruits of economic growth are shared—particularly on what the poor get—and how much the additional resources are used to support public services—particularly primary health care and basic education"(p.17). While recognising the importance of economic growth, the argument suggests that it is not sufficient for ensuring human development. UNDP says: "Today's belated return to human development means reclaiming an old and established heritage rather than importing or implanting a new diversion" (p.14).[1] The Secretary-General of the United Nations, in his report to the General Assembly on *An Agenda for Development* (A/48/935 of 6 May 1994) admitted for the first time: "Less recognised but of deep importance is research in the social sciences; the humanities and the arts. These not only enrich human existence, as has long been recognised, but also are casting new light on many of the essential characteristics and needs of life in the human community in all its many forms"(Boutros-Ghali, 1995:54).

The return to the concern for human development was caused by some disturbing statistics: 20 per cent of the world's population going hungry every night, 25 per cent having no access to safe drinking water, 33 per cent living in a state of abject poverty (with an income of less than a dollar per day), top 20 per cent rich having sixty times the income of the bottom 20 per cent poor, despite declining global military spending it equals nearly the income of the half of humanity—a huge $935 billion dollars is saved with a cut in military expenditure but uncertain use of this peace dividend, spread of narcotic drugs, AIDS pandemic, terrorism and the population explosion that will make this limited globe a habitat for 10 billion people in about five decades from now.

The WSSD endorsed the view that the prevailing paradigm of development that laid excessive reliance on economic growth has failed, that there are deficits in our social development, that culture cannot be pushed aside, that dreaming of a homogenised world is a false and unrealisable dream, and that a holistic approach is needed to tackle the problems of social development rather than sectoral approach followed hitherto. It was a call for people-centred approach. It emphasised the need to think globally but act locally, that is to search solutions that would be relevant, available, and cost-effective. The WSSD put Man in the middle and Culture in the centre.

The common themes that emerged from all the UN conferences held in the last decade of the previous century can be subsumed into four broad categories, as under:

I. *The Enabling Environment*

1. Need for stable macro-economic policy framework.
2. External debt and finance for development.
3. International trade and commodities.
4. Science and technology.

5. Participation, democracy, human rights, accountability and partnership with major groups and non-governmental organisations.
6. Promoting social integration.

II. *Basic Social Services for All*

7. Primary health care, nutrition, education, safe water and sanitation, population and shelter.

III. *Access to Sustainable Livelihoods, Full Employment and Family Incomes*

8. Access to productive occupational opportunities and full employment.
9. Eradication of poverty and hunger.

IV. *Environment and Natural Resources*

It became evident that the new development strategy will have to focus on all these four aspects. Top priority was given to the need for creating an enabling environment at the international level. At the national level, enabling environment got translated into basic services. Thus problems of governance were regarded as crucial to ensure better delivery of social services. One of the major messages of the WSSD was that the United Nations system must develop a united thrust to tackle the problems of social development. The sectoral approach followed hitherto must give way to inter-agency involvement. The UNDP went, as far as, to say that it would redefine its role as "the UN's anti-poverty agency". Soon, the United Nations declared 1996 as the International Year for the Eradication of Poverty, and also decided to dedicate an entire decade to it, beginning 1997.

The Challenge of Poverty

For the first time it happened that all countries of the world acknowledged existence of poverty. It was indeed quite revealing that the socialist countries who strongly denied non-existence of poverty officially accepted its existence after the collapse of communism and in the midst of transition. This was a realisation that neither capitalism nor communism has succeeded in eradicating poverty. Combating poverty required fresh thinking away from stereotypical recipes. It is now agreed that while poverty exists everywhere, it does not have the same etiology. There is not a single "x" factor that causes poverty (y); and poverty itself manifests differently. Talks of "food poverty", "income poverty", and "unhealthy environs" are different facets of the complex phenomenon. We need to delink these partial concepts from the general phenomenon of poverty. It is also important to distinguish between poverty of a given social group and of an individual. Different measures are employed when we talk of poverty of a nation, a poor region within a country, a poor community, a poor family, and a poor person. Similarly, it is necessary to distinguish between the factors that cause poverty in the first instance and the consequences of "living in situations of poverty". Careful studies are needed of both the causes and the consequences of poverty and the interlinkages between them at all the levels of poverty—from an individual to a nation-state or a supra-national region.

Any strategies for the eradication of poverty would need to distinguish between the *poor* and *poverty*. The WSSD left it to the individual countries to develop the criteria for the identification of the poor and poverty, realising that there is no consensus on their definition. However, the WSSD document suggests that the world community was concerned over *absolute* poverty rather than *relative* poverty. The figure of 1.3 billion poor in the world was worked out on that basis regarding those whose income was less than $1 PPP (Purchasing Power Parity) per day. This commitment suggests that those living below this line anywhere need to be salvaged---brought out of the poverty trap. Such an approach is indeed humanitarian and is urgently called for but is not a proper recipe for the more important goal of eradicating poverty. Alleviating the situation of the poor is not the same as eradication of poverty. As John Friedmann and Leonie Sandercock say: "The United Nations figures on poverty...are derived by calculating a 'poverty line' which is expressed in money terms whereby the poor are defined according to their ability (actually inability) to consume. Although household income is sometimes used in surveys, the usual emphasis is on the individual" (1995:14). These authors rightly point out that the emphasis of the old theory of poverty has been on the individual. "According to this theory, the situation of the poor may be improved by increasing the productivity of the labour, by redistribution of income through various forms of subsidies and welfare programmes, and by the (increasingly faint) hope of 'trickle down'" (ibid: 15).

I hold the view that poverty measures should concentrate at the level of the household, which is "both the smallest unit for the self-production of life and livelihood, and the smallest political community". Seen in this perspective, strategies focusing on the individual will have to be reviewed. Leaving aside the non-familial units—that is, the individuals living alone (older individuals deserted by their children, widows, unwed mothers, orphans, disabled and deserted persons)—poverty should be computed at the level of the family/household, and not for each individual separately within a family. By the same token, poverty or riches cannot be gauged through a cumulative index at the level of an ethnic group or caste—neither the rich families within a caste or tribe share their riches with their poorer counterparts nor do they partake in their sufferings caused by the poverty. An ethnic group may consist of large number of poor families but by that token the group does not qualify to be designated as poor. In contrast to this, members in the household share the wealth or the poverty of the household; when they do not, the household gets divided into different households. Both the neo-classical economists and the social welfare oriented politicians have faltered by either focusing on the individual or on a collectivity higher than the household while devising strategies for alleviation of poverty. It is important to distinguish between area-based strategies and household-targeted strategies for the eradication of poverty. An area-based strategy would require focusing on (i) creating an enabling environment ---infrastructural development, provision of community level facilities, linkages with the wider regions etc., and (ii) the poorer households within that area irrespective of caste or race or ethnic considerations. The household targeted strategy, on the other hand, has to focus on the poor households irrespective of their location or their ethnic or caste affiliation. Such a strategy may, or may not, be a part of the area-specific strategy. It would consider a poor a poor without regard to his/her caste or the locale of his/her residence. Both the strategies should, in my view, discard the caste or ethnicity bias and focus on the poor and poverty.

Identifying the Poor and Indexing Poverty

The key question for the social scientists is to evolve a methodology for identifying the poor, and for indexing poverty. To quote Amartya Sen: "The requirements of a concept of poverty must include two distinct---but not unrelated---exercises, namely, (1) a method of identifying a group of people as poor ('identification'); and (2) a method of aggregating the characteristics of the set of poor people into an overall image of poverty ('aggregation')" (1999:11).

Who are poor? There are several ways in which the poor can be identified. Let us discuss some of these criteria and their limitations.

1. *Poor are those who could not meet their daily needs.*

This is the most commonly used criterion. And those using it reduce the concept of daily needs to nutritional requirements usually expressed in terms of calorie intake. While it is a convenient yardstick it is deceptive. There are no standards to define the minimal nutritional requirement. There are people who may be regarded as malnourished but they live long lives and carry out arduous tasks that many well-nourished, coming from the affluent stratum of society, may find difficult to do. Moreover, it is not always possible to translate the nutritional requirement into food requirement. Food intake is governed by the cultural conditioning of an individual and not by objective nutritional value of a food item. A vegetarian cannot be compelled to eat meat to meet his protein needs. If tasteless, an individual would refuse eating cheaper food of high nutritional value. "The actual incomes at which specified nutritional requirements are met will depend greatly on the consumption habits of the people in question" (Sen 1999:12). Malnutrition is just one indicator of poverty, not its composite index.

Moreover, daily minimal needs include items other than food, and it is not easy to specify these requirements as they differ from culture to culture and are affected both by climatic conditions and work habits. What proportion of the income would be spent on food and what on other items is determined by several factors including the inflationary trends, people's choices and availability of the goods and services. The difficulties in using the concept of subsistence minimum in the context of the countries of Eastern Europe—the former communist countries and now classed as "economies-in-transition"----have been enumerated in the chapter devoted to them in this book.

2. *Poor are those who are socially deprived.*

Social deprivation may lead to the downgrading of the social status, and may even adversely affect the economic well-being of the family or the caste, but such a consequence cannot be equated with poverty. And, this for two reasons: (i) poverty may exist among those also who may not be regarded as socially deprived; and (ii) not all those who belong to the category of socially deprived groups---castes or tribes---can be classed as poor. From this view, it will be erroneous to regard the concept of 'Dalit', which has now replaced the Gandhian coinage of 'Harijan' in India, as a synonym of poor. While it is true that those who are covered by this all-embracing term (Dalit) belong to the constitutionally defined cluster of scheduled castes and scheduled tribes that have suffered from alleged neglect and oppression from the upper strata of the society, it would be wrong to equate social inequality with poverty. Lord Krishna belonged to the Yadava caste that now claims a backward status, but he did not belong to the class of the poor; his friend Sudama has been depicted as one living in poverty and he was Brahmin by caste. In the present-day context, one can point finger at a number of so-called Dalit leaders to indicate that no yardstick can place them in the category of the poor. Just as there are both rich and the poor families in any upper caste, so is also the case in any Dalit caste. Thus, not only inequality needs to be distinguished from poverty, but poverty should also be delinked from caste.

Here, it must also be emphasised that it is not only the society of the *Homo Hierarchicus* that exhibits inequality; the *Homo Equalis* societies of the North also have their systems of stratification that generate and perpetuate inequality. It is a different matter whether such inequality is the product of hierarchy or of competition, of ascription or achievement.

Social inequality need not translate into income poverty. And it is income poverty that does create classes of the haves and the have-nots that may, or may not, be based on the fact of birth. It is not only in India that a person "takes birth in debt, lives in debt, and dies in debt passing on the debt burden to his offspring". Culture of poverty exists even in the North in which members get recruited both through birth and inclusion of those who get expelled from other strata.

To quote Sen again: "...inequality is fundamentally a different issue from poverty. To try to analyse poverty 'as an issue of inequality, or the other way round, would do little justice to either. Inequality and poverty are not, of course, unrelated. But neither concept subsumes the other...Neither poverty nor inequality can really be included in the empire of the other" (ibid: 14-15).

3. *Poor are those who feel relatively deprived.*

Several writings on poverty blur the distinction between *relative* and *absolute* poverty. While it has not been so specifically stated, the WSSD's commitment to "eradicate" poverty is with regard to *absolute* poverty and at the level of people. The concept of poverty line or the measure such as $1 (PPP) per capita per day refers to those who are indeed destitute. In terms of relative deprivation, all those whose income is below the average income can be regarded as non-rich, but some countries in Eastern Europe divide them into three categories as indigent, poor and destitute. The destitute are those who cannot meet their daily needs howsoever they may be defined or calculated and need societal and statal intervention to come out of the horrible dead end. Talking of eradication of poverty in the context of destitute implies interventionist policies to ameliorate the situation and introduction of such measures in the country's

> economy and polity that people are prevented from falling into the ditch of absolute poverty. But such measures will not, and cannot, ensure eradication of relative poverty. Theories of social stratification suggest that egalitarianism remains only an ideal; societies wedded to this ideal make efforts to ensure that equality of opportunities is provided to all its citizens but that does not mean that inequalities do not exist in them. Egalitarianism does not rule out competition and the consequent inequalities that are created due to differential performances (of various social actors) and attendant rewards and deprivations. An egalitarian society does not encourage perpetuation of inequalities but is not without inequalities. It attempts to reduce the quantum of relative deprivation and facilitates upward mobility, but it remains stratified.

There is no easy way to define poverty or identify the poor. People can be rendered poor by a variety of factors. Any strategy for the poverty eradication has to be pro-poor and against the phenomenon of poverty. Those who are living in poverty do not constitute a homogeneous group and, therefore, there cannot be a single replicable prescription for the amelioration of their situation. It is, therefore, necessary to first investigate the context in which a given poor resides, identify the source that has caused his/her poverty, inventorise the various deprivations that are suffered as a consequence of poverty and then evolve a strategy that would work in that given context.

From the brief discussion of the problems inherent in defining poverty, it would be clear that there are several manifestations of poverty because it is multifaceted. Let us list the various manifestations of poverty:

1. Poor income and dearth of resources (income poverty). This has four types: (i) absolute income poverty; (ii) low income;

(iii) relative income poverty; and (iv) subjective income poverty.

2. Starvation and malnutrition.
3. Poor health and sanitation causing diseases and decreasing longevity.
4. Lack of access to education and other related facilities. In the community context, it may mean non-existence of a school in the neighbourhood; but for a household it may also mean lack of paying capacity for sending a child to school.
5. Homelessness—people without homes; or the community with poor housing such as slums. People can be rendered homeless because of a natural disaster such as an earthquake or a typhoon and may not be in a position to incur expenses in building a shelter for them. Even the well-to-do can become pauper because of disasters—natural or man-made.
6. Unsafe environment.
7. Social exclusion and negative discrimination.

The above listing would suggest that poverty could be caused not only by low income but also by non-availability of, or denial of access to, other facilities and services. Poverty can be caused both at the level of a community or nation, and at the level of the individual family by population growth. Similarly, needless consumption and wrong economic policies also affect resources and the environment and impoverish both the family and the community. Urbanisation and migration have also been identified as contributory factors to poverty at both the levels. Poverty is, thus, a complex and multidimensional problem that defies any simple solutions. Most of the strategies that are proposed and practised are in the nature of charity, a tokenism from the non-poor to the non-rich. It is more in the nature of a clinical approach of a quack who administers medicine to the patient for relief from a visible pain. Such a treatment may give immediate relief but will not reach the real source of the ailment that may require thorough investigation and diagnosis, and later a surgical intervention.

The poor perform useful functions for the society which the rich fight shy of doing themselves. Such tasks are functionally important but have a lower valuation in terms of rewards. Domestic help, cleaning the streets and scavenging, and removal of night soil are all regarded as dirty and menial jobs which the poor willingly undertake to earn their living. It is alleged that hierarchical societies kept such oppressed people away from climbing the ladder of social prestige so that they continue providing these services. Secondly, the poor are needed to buy second-hand or rejected goods and items of food, and to avail of the services of relatively incompetent teachers and doctors; in the absence of the poor buyers such goods and services will remain unsold. It is for the same reasons that many petro-rich countries of the Middle East encouraged migration of the poor people from the Asian region. The cheap salaries given to them were higher compared to what they were earning in their parent countries, but were, in fact, relatively far less than what the host countries would be offering to their own compatriots for the same set of services. Politicians need the poor to serve as their vote bank.

Scholars researching on poverty have come round the view that every society lives two interacting but separate cultures, namely, the culture of the rich and the culture of poverty. The poverty of the people also affects the non-poor and their involvement in any programme for the eradication of poverty is essential. Not only the rich feel that the poor are an economic burden, they also have vested interest in keeping the poor poor to run the economy. Some of the critics of the failure of planning in many developing countries have even argued that the rise in poverty despite developmental programmes may appear as failure in terms of the *manifest objectives*, but such a consequence could as well be a part of their *latent*, unstated, hidden agenda. In the name of the poor, these plans and policies might have been designed to benefit the rich. Poverty programmes are regarded as a conspiracy of the non-poor. In the early seventies---more than two decades after India attained its independence---when the then Prime Minister of India, Indira Gandhi, raised afresh the slogan of *Garibi Hatao,* people wondered whether it was an acknowledgement of the failure of the Congress government to remove poverty all those years, or such a call was just another political gimmick to entice the poor and earn their voting support. In later days, two other Prime Ministers---Rajiv Gandhi and Atal Behari Vajpayee---went on record to admit that only a minor portion of the total allocation meant for the poor really reaches them. The intermediaries, including the politicians and the bureaucracy, usurp a major portion of the developmental aid.

It is interesting to note that while all share the rhetoric of eradicating poverty, there exist vested interests both among the poor and the non-poor in perpetuating poverty. If the non-poor want poverty to perpetuate for the above-mentioned reasons, the poor have a vested interest in being regarded as poor to take advantage of the state-sponsored policies of "positive discrimination". Such vested interest in remaining "poor" or "least developed" or even "developing" is demonstrated even by the countries. Such countries do not wish to be declassed. When in the 1980s the international community proposed to encourage "endogenous development" many countries from the so-called "Third World" saw in it the conspiracy of the North to withdraw their developmental aid. Similarly, many countries refuse to employ the World Bank concept of Purchasing Power Parity (PPP) in place of US dollars (without PPP adjustment) to express its GNP per capita for fear of moving out of the list of developing countries.

World Summit for Social Development Guidelines for Eradicating Poverty

Meeting in such a global scenario of rampant poverty, the World Summit for Social Development (WSSD), held in March 1995, made this commitment in its declaration:

> We commit ourselves to the goal of eradicating poverty in the world, through decisive national actions and international cooperation, as an ethical, social, political and economic imperative of humankind.
>
> To this end, at the national level, in partnership with all actors of civil society and in the context of a multidimensional and integrated approach, we will
>
> a. formulate or strengthen, as a matter of urgency, and preferably by the year 1996, the International Year for the Eradication of Poverty, national policies and strategies geared to substantially reducing overall poverty in the shortest possible time, reducing inequalities and eradicating absolute poverty by a target date to be specified by each country in its national context;
>
> b. focus our efforts and policies to address the root causes of poverty and to provide for the basic needs of all. These efforts should include the elimination of hunger and malnutrition; the provision of food security, education, employment and livelihood, primary health care, safe drinking water and sanitation, and adequate shelter; and participation in social and cultural life. Special priority will be given to the needs and rights of women and children, who often bear the greatest burden of poverty, and to the needs of vulnerable and disadvantaged groups and persons;
>
> c. ensure that people living in poverty have access to productive resources, including credit, land, education and training, technology, knowledge and information, as well as to public services, and participate in decision-making on a

policy and regulatory environment that would enable them to benefit from expanding employment and economic opportunities;

d. develop and implement policies to ensure that all people have adequate economic and social protection during unemployment, ill health, maternity, child-rearing, widowhood, disability and old age;

e. ensure that national budgets and policies are oriented, as necessary, to meeting basic needs, reducing inequalities and targeting poverty, as a strategic objective; and

f. seek to reduce inequalities, increase opportunities and access to resources and income, and remove any political, legal, economic and social factors and constraints that foster and sustain inequality.

The WSSD focused on the people living in poverty and emphasised the need for reducing inequalities, eradicating absolute poverty and ensuring provision of basic needs for all. Thus, poverty strategies are expected to have a three-pronged approach. The steps relative to the eradication of absolute poverty should be seen as a fire-fighting approach. The state and the civil society are expected to take actions to provide for the basic needs of the absolutely poor, and also ensure that they have access to the facilities denied to them so far. The strategy should be such that helps the poor to come out of the poverty trap and prevent others (particularly the vulnerable groups such as women, children and the older people) from falling into it. If inequalities and the denial of access to basic facilities cause or further reinforce poverty, it is necessary to take corrective actions that would help reduce inequalities and ensure access to basic facilities and services.

The Programme of Action, proposed by WSSD to honour the commitment to eradicate poverty, has focused on ten points.[2] These are:

1. National policies ought to be formulated to considerably reduce the incidence of poverty while fixing a target date that is regarded nationally feasible.
2. Support may be sought of international organisations in the national efforts to eradicate poverty.
3. Tools be developed to measure different types of poverty in a given country context, and immediate relief be provided to those groups that are in high-risk category.
4. Economic policies and national budgets should be regularly reviewed and amended as necessary to meet the objective of poverty eradication.
5. Opportunities may be expanded to enable the poor people to enhance their overall capacities and improve their social and economic conditions, ensuring sustainability of resources.
6. Emphasis may be laid on human resource development and improvement of infrastructural facilities.
7. There must be a comprehensive provision for the basic needs of all.
8. Adequate economic and social protection may be provided to all during periods of unemployment, ill-health, maternity, disability and old age.
9. Policies may be formulated to strengthen the family and contribute to its stability.
10. To assist poverty-stricken areas all resources---public and private---be mobilised and involvement of the civil society may be ensured.

It need not be stressed that poverty excludes and marginalises people. The high degree of illiteracy, malnutrition and ill-health, and general neglect suffered by the poor results in their having an indifference towards the society and the polity. Economic marginalisation leads to civic and political marginalisation. The answer, therefore, is seen in the mobilisation of the poor, and in their empowerment. While according the highest priority to the alleviation of poverty in all South Asian countries, the 1991 Colombo Summit of the SAARC Heads of State suggested this strategy. To quote from the text of the Summit Declaration:

> They affirmed that South Asia's poor could constitute a huge and potential resource provided their basic needs are met and they are mobilized to create economic growth. This requires that the poor are empowered and are irreversibly linked to the mainstream of development. It was noted that each South Asian country has had significant success cases of this approach to poverty alleviation.
>
> Recognising that a great majority of these people remain below the poverty line, they evinced keen interest in a "Daal-Bhaat" or assured nutritional standards approach towards the satisfaction of basic needs of the South Asian poor.
>
> Deeply conscious that primary education is the cutting edge in the struggle against poverty and the promotion of development, the Heads of State or Government reaffirmed the importance of attaining the target of providing primary education to all the children between the ages of 6-14 years by the year 2000. They agreed to share their respective experiences and technical expertise to achieve this goal.

These are standard recipes. One can add some more to the list of panaceas offered by the experts and policy makers. There is need to examine the applicability of each of these prescriptions in the specific context. While poverty is a global phenomenon, there are no global, that is, universally applicable, solutions to eradicate this persistent obstinacy. The old and established theories of poverty have been challenged by the "discovery" of poverty in the countries that had earlier denied its presence. Poverty in the countries of the former Soviet bloc is not the same as poverty in the countries of the North; and is certainly very different from the poverty that prevails in the countries of the South located in Africa, Latin America, Asia and the Pacific. Of course, everywhere, the destitute, the absolute poor, need help from whatever source it can arrive to overcome starvation and own a shelter to protect themselves from the vagaries of nature. For such people, empowerment is a far cry, maybe a long-term goal, but not an immediate agenda. Not all prescriptions suit every class of the poor and at every stage of poverty.

Time has come to investigate the situation of the poor in concrete settings going beyond the macro-statistics based on measurable but partial indicators so that reliable profiles of the poor can be prepared and their needs can be properly prioritised. Dumping the discarded or surplus goods in the colonies of the poor may appear to be a humanitarian act, but it may create more problems than solve the plight of the poor. Instances abound where cans of dry milk powder provided under the auspices of the UNICEF found their way in the market of the non-poor and the children of the poor continued to remain malnourished. Big size western clothes sent to the earthquake-devastated area or the flood-affected people found no takers among the victims of natural hazards: what use mini-skirts could have for women who wear sarees? Sending books and stationery within days of an earthquake disaster is a sure guarantee that such a philanthropic gesture shall remain unnoticed. All these are instances of misplaced mercies. Some of them may help alleviate poverty but certainly not empower the poor.

These days, *empowerment* has become a key word and is employed freely with total endorsement from everyone. Anyone contradicting it faces the prospect of being dubbed as reactionary, anti secular, and anti-poor. But, despite its overuse, the concept remains vaguely defined and the word is used more as a synonym for many things—providing education, participation in voting and in protests and demonstrations, entering the job market, good health, human rights, and so on. It is in such a milieu that the role of the civil society has also been highlighted. Again, differences exist in regard to the definition of this concept, and also about the precise expectations from this section of the society.

In countries where the poor constitute a majority, one wonders about the nature of a civil society. No doubt, the silence of the poor also speaks, but one doubts whether it is heard. And even if it is heard, whether it is heeded. There are also the *middlemen* who speak on behalf of the poor, and speak quite forcefully. It still remains to be found out what is the ultimate consequence of all that serious and well-intended effort. Poverty has not gone, and the ranks of the poor are constantly inflating. The poor will have to learn to break their silence, to give up their dependence on the middlemen, and to assert that they belong to the centre and not to the margins. In other words, a true civil society will come only when the large constituency of the poor is empowered. Why is it not happening? What are the obstacles? What are the implementable strategies for their inclusion, or their assertion for inclusion? These are the questions that we must ask and we must find answers.

Poverty offers a challenge for effective social science research that goes beyond official statistics and journalistic portrayals. It is just not enough to find out the *exact* number of the poor, or to determine the "poverty line", or even to construct the "Human Development Index (HDI)". These are good and elegant exercises and serve some useful purposes but are not enough to tackle the problem of poverty or ameliorate the situation of the poor. There is a need to go beyond the set prescriptions, and piecemeal approaches. Neither the reforms in the economy, nor eradication of illiteracy or universalisation of primary education, nor even the functioning of democracy be regarded as prophylactic for the occurrence of poverty; by the same token, they cannot also be used as a curative medicine for this complex ailment.

The new research on poverty should ask questions such as: Is poverty an attribute of underdeveloped societies? Can development provide a cure? If yes, then, what kind of development? What are different causes of poverty and what are different manifestations of it? Is there any relationship between the cause of poverty and its manifestation? In other words, can poverty manifest differently though caused by the same factor; and can poverty of similar manifestation be caused by a variety of factors in different settings and in the same setting at different points of time? Does the manifestation of poverty show its gravity or indicate its distinctive character?

The recent focus on poverty has shown that in individual countries poverty is caused by (i) paucity of resources or by failure of economic development; (ii) failure of the state; and (iii) transition from state-controlled economy to market-based economy. In earlier periods, even slavery and indentured labour caused poverty. The need is to first identify the poor families and the poor geographical areas and then to carry out systematic investigations with an open mind to understand the phenomenon of poverty and adjudge the strategies employed to combat it. This will help both in building a new theoretical perspective of an interdisciplinary character and in developing a dependable portfolio for affirmative action and prophylactic treatment.

Notes

1. No one knows better than I about the bias of the UN system in favour of the "economic". As Regional Adviser for Social Sciences in Asia and the Pacific for long eighteen years I tried my very best to earn a funding support from the UNDP for the promotion of social sciences in developing countries of this vast region, but had no success; even when one of the regional projects proposed by my office got into their so-called "ward robe" after careful scrutiny—which I had no means to influence—it was surreptitiously dropped at the final stage on a pretext that I never could understand. It was hard to imagine an agency dedicated to development mostly manned by those trained in social sciences so ruthlessly subverting the cause of social sciences. And, it is the same agency now talking of return to the old concern of the social sciences. We can only hope that there has been a change of the mindset in that organization; but that remains to be seen
2. In the Appendix to this book the Programme of Action recommended by the WSSD is reproduced in full.

References

Boutros-Ghali, Boutros, 1995, *An Agenda for Development* (with related UN Documents). New York: United Nations.

Friedmann, John and Leonie Sandercock, 1995, "Empowerment: An Escape route from Poverty" in *UNESCO Courier,* March 1995 issue on DEVELOPMENT: The Haves and Have-nots.

SAARC, 1992, *Meeting the Challenge: Report of the Independent South Asian Commission on Poverty Alleviation.* SAARC Secretariat, Kathmandu.

Sen, Amartya, 1999 (paperback edition), original in 1981, *Poverty and Famines*. New Delhi: Oxford University Press.

UNDP, 1995, *Poverty Eradication: A Policy Framework for Country Strategies.* New York: Bureau for Policy and Programme Support, UNDP.

UNESCO, 1996, *UNESCO and the World Summit for Social Development* (ed. Yogesh Atal). Paris: Sector for Social and Human Sciences, UNESCO.

2

Poverty in Transition and Transition in Poverty

We commit ourselves to the goal of eradicating poverty in the world, through decisive national actions and international cooperation, as an ethical, social, political, and economic imperative of humankind.

—Commitment # 2, *Declaration* by the *World Summit for Social Development*

We have used our wealth and knowledge to explore space and reach the moon, while failing to reach poor neighbourhoods and ghettos. These people are reachable, but remain unreached.

We must commit ourselves to the geographically remote and socially distant... As we strive to build superhighways, we must not forget the streets and blind alleys where a vast segment of humanity lives in a constricted world, suffering from hunger, indignities, and neglect.

—Federico Mayor
Director-General of UNESCO, 17 October 1995

This is introduction to the book *Poverty in Transition and Transition in Poverty* edited by Yogesh Atal and published jointly by UNESCO and Berghahn Books, New York, 1999.

Prologue

Preparing to enter the twenty-first century, and looking back at the gains of the past fifty years of developmental efforts, the world community has engaged itself in reprioritising its agenda. There is certainly a feeling of satisfaction over the achievements made, but there is also a realisation that much remains to be done. The development path pursued in the past five decades has not only failed to achieve some of its goals, but has also contributed to the inventory of problems. We need to attend to the unfinished agenda, and to address the newly emerging problems of global dimension. We have acknowledged the fact that despite growing modernisation and gains in terms of economic growth most countries of the world---both developing and developed---have faltered on the social front and have ignored environmental concerns while pursuing economic growth. Irrespective of the political system, and notwithstanding economic development, there are deficiencies in social development everywhere. All societies confront the problems of rising poverty, growing unemployment and ruptures in social integration. The World Summit for Social Development was convened to focus on these issues and to seek the commitment of world leadership to make a united effort to resolve them alongside the implementation of Agenda 21 adopted at the Rio Earth Summit. The road from Rio to Copenhagen helped expand the concept of sustainability by including social and cultural concerns; it was a move towards the integration of ecology and sociology.

"What if the environment is saved and cultures are lost?" was as important a concern as "what if cultures are saved and the environment is deteriorated?" The two could not be seen apart from each other. Fusion of these twin concerns highlighted the need for a holistic approach to replace the economic orientation. The Copenhagen Summit called for an approach that would facilitate the search for solutions that are culturally rooted and ecologically sustainable. It endorsed the view that economic growth alone cannot ensure all-round development.

Traditional development strategies were based on the trickle-down theory and ignored the human factor. They failed to address the fundamental imbalances in society and, thus, did not make any significant impact on poverty eradication. We have now realised that economic growth alone is not enough to ensure social development. Economic growth should be so planned that it serves the cause of social development rather than creating crises in the social sphere.

The Copenhagen message was loud and clear. There are common problems---problems that prevail in all societies, in the South or North, East or West; but there are no common solutions. The paradigm of development that was pursued in the Third World led to as much of frustration on the social front as the paradigm adopted by the socialist world. The collapse of communism, and the growing disenchantment with the development paradigm in the Third World, gave a clear signal that neither of these is appropriate for addressing the task of social development. Additionally, the presence of the problems of poverty, unemployment, and of tendencies toward social disintegration in the so-called developed world suggests that even these countries do not have an answer; they too are in search of solutions. Despite a high rating on all the indicators of development—economic growth, high industrialisation, total literacy, better health, and a democratic system---if these countries are also in deep social crisis then it is necessary to find out what else is needed to overcome these problems. We have reached a stage in which all countries are engulfed in social crises and in which there are no ready-made solutions for overcoming them. We live in a world of similar problems but of dissimilar opportunities.

Poverty is a problem with global dimensions. Reports on the world social situation hint at the rising numbers of the poor. It is generally believed that the number of the poor has already crossed the one billion mark. Standing at 1.3 billion, the number of poor today is greater than that of adult illiterates, which is around 800 million. In fact, the number of poor is much larger, as most of the figures regarding the size of the poor population, given in official publications, relate only to the developing world.[1] Poverty was officially denied in the socialist world until the collapse of the Soviet Union, and so data on poverty in those countries during that period are not available. Now that the existence of poverty is accepted even officially, statistics are being collected, but they are still not very satisfactory.[2]

Since most of the poor inhabit the so-called Third World—an appellation that has become redundant after the collapse of the socialist world—more statistics and better analyses of poverty in those countries are available. However, it must be said that most of these studies and reports are official accounts, or analyses carried out within the framework of macro-economics. In-depth sociological studies of the poor in different socio-cultural settings are still scattered. There are several poverty groups that have not been studied, and there are several anti-poverty measures being taken without a proper empirical base. Application of set recipes is still the norm.

The designation of 1996 as the International Year for the Eradication of Poverty (IYEP), and the decade 1997-2006 as the International Decade for the Eradication of Poverty by the United Nations—following the recommendation of the Copenhagen World Summit—is a clear indication of the priority assigned to poverty by the world community. It is significant that the Copenhagen Summit preferred the word "eradication" to "alleviation," because it regarded the prevalence and growth of poverty as totally "unacceptable" and wanted the United Nations system, as well as member-states, to make a concerted effort to erase this scourge by attacking its root causes, not just providing relief to those who live in poverty. There is, thus, an increase in governmental concern over poverty and a commitment on the part of the United Nations system to contribute to the eradication of poverty. But, the academic research, particularly by domestic specialists, that is needed to support these initiatives is still very meagre and not very dependable. The indigenous social science community has to undertake the tasks of developing suitable theoretical paradigms, of innovating new methodologies, and of coming up with policy-relevant findings and recommendations. So far, much of the impetus has come from outside agencies and foreign researchers. But external intervention, not based on a deeper understanding of the local situation, cannot substitute for insider insights. There is an urgent need to stimulate social scientific research on the phenomenon of poverty in different parts of the world, focusing primarily on those areas and groups that have not been studied. And, in this task, the involvement of indigenous scholars must be secured so that they contribute both to the theory and methodology of poverty research, as well as to social policy in their respective countries. Such research, carried out by indigenous researchers, would ensure that culture-specific solutions will be found for the problems in place of borrowed solutions from abroad, which have generally ignored the cultural factor and thus failed to deliver.

Poverty is a multidimensional phenomenon and is caused by a variety of factors. Its manifestations also differ from context to context. There is no linear chain of cause and effect: an interrelated web of economic, social, psychological, cultural and political factors influence the occurrence and persistence of poverty. Real poverty may not be apparent, and apparent poverty may not be real. Thus, there cannot be a single strategy to eradicate it in different societal contexts. In order to develop realistic national strategies for poverty eradication, it is of utmost importance that these be based on an objective appraisal of the etiology of poverty, its spread, and its pathology. For this, we need to take country-based stock of existing research and studies, including official reports and analyses, and to make an evaluation of the various antipoverty measures and policy initiatives. Such an exercise would help us identify the research gaps that exist, and also learn lessons from past experience about what went wrong and what should be prioritised.

As a follow-up to the World Summit for Social Development, and as a contribution to the International Decade for the Eradication of Poverty, UNESCO encouraged a review of national strategies toward poverty eradication. For the Asia-Pacific region, it supported the initiative of the Association of Asia-Pacific Social Science Research Councils (AASSREC) for a regional cross-cultural project on environment and poverty. For the region of Eastern Europe, including other countries that formerly belonged to the Soviet bloc, it decided to invite national scholars from a select number of countries to prepare profiles of poverty and evaluate current social policies and programmes on poverty eradication. These studies were published in a book titled *Poverty in Transition and Transition in Poverty* (ed. Yogesh Atal, UNESCO and Berghahn books, 1999). In order to provide a comparative perspective and to ensure a wider dissemination of this important research effort, this essay was written as an "Introduction" to that book.

Countries-in-Transition: From No Poverty to Poverty

The focus on poverty in the countries-in-transition belonging to the former Soviet bloc is of particular importance. As mentioned earlier, during the socialist period, these countries officially denied the existence of poverty. Making the transition from capitalism to socialism, they nourished the hope of completely terminating all oppression and all forms of social inequality to fulfil the Marxist dream. Feeling frustrated, these countries are now experiencing a reverse transition—from socialism to capitalism. Just as the entry into the era of socialism raised hopes amongst the masses of an emerging egalitarian society, the collapse of communism has caused a similar euphoria; people are hoping that all the troubles of the past will dissipate and sudden riches will appear. While there was an awareness of some of the social costs involved in this process of transition, the massive drops in output and income, which have caused large-scale unemployment and an upsurge in poverty were hardly anticipated.

Countries that denied the existence of poverty and unemployment in the past, and that boasted of high literacy rates and skilled manpower, are now acknowledging not only the prevalence of poverty but its sudden and rapid increase. "Eastern Europe and the countries of the Commonwealth of Independent States (CIS) have seen the greatest deterioration in the past decade. Income poverty has spread from a small part of their population to about a third—120 million people below a poverty line of $4 a day," says the 1997 UNDP Human Development Report. "The transition from socialism to democracy and market economies has proved more difficult and costly than anyone imagined. The costs have been not only economic, from the dramatic decline in GDP. They have also been human, from falling wages, growing crime, and loss of social protection. In some countries life expectancy has fallen by five years or more" (UNDP 1997: 3). Such a situation challenges the existing theories on poverty and calls for a re-examination of the relationship between education, unemployment and poverty. In poor countries, unemployment is usually the phenomenon of the middle class as the poor cannot afford to remain unemployed. It is a different matter, however, that in the long run the unemployed may become poor. In the countries-in-transition, most of the currently unemployed are those who have lost their jobs due to the restructuring of the economy. And these are people who are educated and mostly skilled. Furthermore, the reduction in state social assistance and benefits has caused difficulties both for pensioners and new job seekers.

Careful sociological investigation is needed to understand the phenomenon of poverty in these countries. Is it a new form of poverty that is emerging, or is it suppressed poverty that is resurfacing? During the socialist era, a distinction was made between the *capitalist poor* and the *socialist poor.* The capitalist poor were those who had been victims of the previous capitalist system and as such were given priority consideration in the new system for the amelioration of their situation. The socialist poor were the victims of the new system, such as the handicapped, the vagrants, and people with temporary jobs. The latter were never regarded as poor by communist ideologues; they were considered as mere "aberrations". To quote Milanovic: "Poverty was not only viewed as social pathology and an explicit denial of the 'perfectness' of the system but... rather sinisterly, as an explicit *antisocial choice* by the poor" (n.d.: 4). That is the reason why poverty was never studied in that part of the world. To quote yet another author, Alastair McAuley: "In Soviet eyes, socialism was a progressive ideology... Party propagandists liked to claim that, certainly by the 1960s, the USSR had made considerable strides toward the goal of creating a just and equal society. As a result, it was suggested that there could be no poverty. Furthermore, if there was no poverty, there could be no justification for the academic study of the phenomenon" (1996:355). However, the "growing economic crisis that preceded the collapse of state socialism and the breakup of the USSR was accompanied by a growth in poverty—and a belated recognition on the part of the Soviet government that poverty existed in the USSR. The transition to a market economy has been accompanied by an enormous further increase in poverty in Russia and, indeed, in most of the other successor states of the former Soviet Union (FSU)" (ibid:354). The present effort at understanding the emerging phenomenon of poverty, thus, assumes special significance.

It would have been ideal to cover all the countries that once constituted the so-called Second World. However, neither the resources nor the time were available to launch such an ambitious project. Instead, it was decided to select some representative cases and have them studied by indigenous scholars rather than by "outsiders". The proposal was explained to eight regional UNESCO National Commissions, and their support was requested in identifying scholars who would carry out the studies, broadly following the outlines provided by UNESCO. Six of these countries responded promptly and identified scholars, who were then contacted. The countries covered by this study are: Bulgaria, Georgia, Hungary, Mongolia, Romania, and the Russian Federation. This is a rather fortunate composition as these countries represent different parts of the region that constituted the Soviet bloc, as shown below:

Central Europe	Hungary
Southeastern Europe	Bulgaria, Romania
Caucasian Republic	Georgia
Western part of the former Soviet Union	Russian Federation
Far Eastern	Mongolia

Together these six countries represent 197.4 million of the world's population. Their GNP per capita ranges from US $310 (Mongolia) to US $4,120 (Hungary). In all these countries the average annual growth rate during the decade 1985-95 has been negative, ranging between -1.1 per cent (Hungary) and -17 per cent (Georgia). In Romania, 17.7 per cent of the population lives below the poverty line, having less than $1 a day, Purchasing Power Parity (PPP), to live on. Table 1 provides a summary view of basic indicators culled from the World Bank Report in these six countries.

Table 1
The Chosen Countries: A Comparative Profile

Indicators	*Bulgaria*	*Georgia*	*Hungary*	*Mongolia*	*Romania*	*Russia*
Population (millions)	8.4	5.4	10.2	2.5	22.7	148.2
Surface area (1,000 sq. kms.)	111	70	93	1,567	238	17,075
GNP per capita (1995 U.S.$)	1,330	440	4,120	310	1,480	2,240
Annual growth (%) 1985-95	-2.6	-17	-1.0	-3.8	-3.8	-5.1
PPP estimates of GNP per capita						
1987	23.4	28.1	28.9	10.6	22.2	30.9
1995	16.6	5.5	23.8	7.2	16.2	16.61
Current int'l (1995 U.S.$)	4,480	1,574	6,410	1,950	4,360	4,480
Poverty (percent of people living on less than $1 a day [PPP])	2.6		0.7		17.7	1.1
Life expectancy at birth 1995	71	73	70	65	70	65

It should be stressed that the structure of poverty in Eastern Europe is radically different from that of the developing countries. In the latter, while the actual number of poor is still on the rise, their percentage compared to the total population is declining. As a result, the poverty gap is also being somewhat reduced. The situation in Eastern Europe is quite the opposite: an increase is registered on all the indicators (see Table 2 for these comparisons).

Table 2

Growth of Poverty in Eastern Europe and the Developing Countries

Indicators	*Years*	*Eastern Europe*	*Developing countries*
Number of poor (in millions)	1987	2	1,225
	1990	n.a.	1,261
	1993	15	1,299
Head count index	1987	0.6%	33.3%
	1990	n.a.	32.9
	1993	3.5	31.8
Poverty gap	1987	0.2	10.8
	1990	n.a.	10.3
	1993	1.1	10.5

Measuring Poverty: Concepts and Methods

While there is a worldwide concern about the growth and spread of poverty, and an acknowledgment of its existence in practically all the countries---developed or developing, capitalist or former socialist---there is no unanimity as regards its definition. People regarded poor in a given country may be considered rich when measured by the yardstick of another country. The definition given by "outsiders" may not be acceptable to those who are being defined; and similarly, self-perception may contrast with outside observation, or even statistical indexing. Since poverty is said to be multidimensional, a monetary measure of poverty may not be a reliable way to determine poverty, or classify a person as poor. Moreover, all the poor cannot be classed in a single category. We already referred to a distinction made in the former socialist countries between the capitalist poor and the socialist poor---the latter regarded as a contradiction in terms, as an aberration. Differentiation is also made between those who are hereditarily poor, for whom poverty is an *ascribed* status, and those who are the "new poor", for whom poverty is an *achieved* status. Again, the new poor do not constitute a single homogeneous group. The political refugees and the environmental refugees have something in common: they both had to flee from their habitat and seek refuge elsewhere; but the amelioration of their situation would need different strategies. The new poor, in the countries-in-transition—the subject matter of the present study, are neither the illiterate, nor the continuing unemployed; they are mainly the job-dislocated people, those who are paid low wages, or those whose wages/salaries have been deferred, making it extremely difficult for the family to feed its members.

Difficulties in defining poverty have been aptly summed up in the 1997 UNDP Human Development Report thus:

> Concerns with identifying people affected by poverty and the desire to measure it have at times obscured the fact that poverty is too complex to be reduced to a single dimension of human life. It has become common for countries to establish an income-based or consumption-based poverty line. Although income focuses on an important dimension of poverty, it gives only a partial picture of the many ways human lives can be blighted. Someone can enjoy good health and live quite long but be illiterate and thus cut off from learning, from communication and from interactions with others. Another person may be literate and quite well educated but prone to premature death because of epidemiological characteristics or physical disposition. Yet a third may be excluded from participating in the important decision-making processes affecting her life. The deprivation of none of them can be fully captured by the level of their income (pp.15-16).

Three distinct approaches are recognised by UNDP for the treatment of poverty. The *income perspective* focuses on the level of income of a person or family, and sets limits to draw a poverty line. The *basic needs perspective* views poverty from the angle of material deprivation rather than by income. A person or family is considered poor if it is not able to provide for minimally acceptable basic needs. The *capability perspective* focuses on the functionings that a person can or cannot achieve, given the opportunities s/he has. Functionings refer to the various valuable things a person can do or be, such as living long, being healthy, being well-nourished, mixing well with others in the community and so on. The *human development approach* to poverty adopted in the UNDP Human Development Report draws on each of these perspectives, but draws particularly on the capability perspective (UNDP 1997: 15-16).

The Human Poverty Index (HPI), introduced by UNDP in its 1997 Human Development Report, "uses indicators of the most basic dimensions of deprivation: a short life, lack of basic education and lack of access to public and private resources" (UNDP 1997: 5). "The variables used are the percentage of people expected to die before age 40, the percentage of adults who are illiterate, and overall economic provisioning in terms of percentage of people without access to health services and safe water and the percentage of underweight children under five" (ibid: 14). The UNDP has computed this index for only seventy-eight developing countries. It is obvious that computation of this index for the countries-in-transition is not possible due to the absence of adequate data, and also, perhaps due to the non-applicability of these indicators in defining poverty in those regions, for the same reasons as advanced for the industrialised countries. Since Mongolia is classified as a developing country, however, its HPI is computed: its HPI value is shown as 15.7 per cent, ranking sixteenth and implying that about one-sixth of its people suffer from human poverty. This ranking is incidentally higher than India (36.7%) or Indonesia (20.8%). At the bottom of the list are seven countries whose HPI exceeds 50 per cent: Niger, Sierra Leone, Burkina Faso, Ethiopia, Mali, Cambodia, and Mozambique (ibid: 21).

Since the measures of poverty employed in other developing countries are not suited to the situation prevalent in the countries-in-transition, the governments of these countries, as well as the scholars, employ the same standards that were used during the previous regimes—of course with some needed modifications. Rather than dividing people in terms of income, which is a measure for identifying relative poverty, the aim of these measures was to find out whether the income earned by the individual, or the family/household, was sufficient to meet basic needs. It may be recalled that in the socialist regimes, income inequality was minimised to the maximum, and minimum wages were fixed in terms of basic needs to ensure that nobody suffered from privation. With the arrival of differences in income due to the introduction of the market economy, the same measure is used to demarcate the poverty line.

The following is a list of some of the concepts employed in poverty research in these countries.

The concept of the *poverty line* is also used here, but in a somewhat different sense. We know that this line differs from country to country depending upon the definition and the criteria used to delineate it. For making international comparisons, the World Bank decided to use US $1 (PPP) a day as the demarcation line: families spending one US dollar a day or less are regarded as living below the poverty line. However, for the countries-in-transition, US $4 was considered to be the appropriate line by the UNDP.

In countries-in-transition, a different technique is used to draw the poverty line. It is drawn in relation to average income. For example, in Russia, all the people who receive less than the average income are regarded as living below the poverty line. However, these people are grouped into three categories depending on the distance between the average income and their own income. Immediately below them are the *indigents,* followed by the *poor* and the *destitute.* The indigents are those whose income is between 50 and 75 per cent of the average income; the poor are those whose income is between 25 and 50 per cent of the average income; and the destitute, leading a life of misery, are those whose income is less than 25 per cent of the average income. Some scholars also follow the OECD procedure for drawing the poverty line at 50, 60 or 70 per cent of the average income level. In both cases, it is the money income which is the measure, irrespective of its PPP value.

A more refined method is the computation of the *subsistence minimum*—a concept of the old Soviet methodology. This is also calculated in different ways. Some determine it in terms of the *food basket.* For each member of the household, an appropriate number of calories are allocated depending on the person's age and sex, and then the cost of food items equivalent to those calories is calculated. Thus, the total amount of money needed to buy food for the family, satisfying the calorie norm, is defined as the subsistence minimum. The standards set by the Food and Agricultural Organisation (FAO) and the World Health Organisation (WHO) are also employed for this purpose; these standards indicate the calorie value of each food item. This method is criticised on the grounds that people eat food not only for its calorific value but also for taste and cultural prescriptions. As such, the computation must be done on the basis of what people really eat, and not on what they should eat. However, people using this measure fix subsistence minimum differently for different regions because of the differences in the price of food items. Using this technique, the subsistence minimum for the Soviet Union, before its collapse, was fixed at 190 rubles per capita per month, which was more than US $220 at 1990 exchange rates. Accordingly, 11.4 per cent of the population was identified as poor. This figure rose to 31 per cent in 1993 at the 1990 price standard based on PPP.

In Hungary, the concept of subsistence minimum is further divided into two categories: *social minimum* and *survival minimum.* "The *social minimum is* the income necessary to fulfill basic necessities, allowing for the consumption of goods and services desired by the general public, albeit of a modest but socially acceptable level and quality" (Szalai 1990: 297). The *survival minimum* is 80-85 percent of the social minimum. It is expressed as "an income which allows only a very modest fulfillment of basic necessities connected with a daily life routine" (ibid). The Hungarian author, however, warns that "the poverty line is not a 'neutral' form of measurement" in the Hungarian context. "In Hungary, the calculation determining the poverty line emerged, not in political debates, but by a decision of the Political Committee of the Communist Party in 1983." The poverty line was determined with an agreement on the extent to which poverty "should be admitted... The poverty lines calculated for various social groups still do not serve as a legal basis to guaranteeing these groups the necessary welfare benefits" (ibid).

In Bulgaria, a distinction is made between the *social minimum* and the *living minimum,* much along the same lines as in Hungary. The social minimum in Bulgaria defines the "upper line of poverty," while the living minimum defines the lower line. Those who come under the first category are relatively better-off as they are able to spend something on "comforts"; but the living minimum does not provide access to goods other than the bare necessities of life.

In Romania, three different measures are used, namely, *Subsistence Minimum* (SM), *Decent Minimum of Life* (DM), and *Minimum Determined by the Ministry of Labour and Social Protection* (MM). The SM, in the Romanian context, is said to refer to "absolute" poverty, to draw the poverty line (but here absolute poverty is not synonymous with destitution). The DM is equivalent to an average wage; it is used to define "relative" poverty. The MM is a value obtained for households whose income is below the SM and DM. Taking DM as a standard, SM is defined as 59.9 per cent of the DM; those who get 31.5 per cent of the DM, or 52.6 per cent of the SM, are put in the category of MM. These people are considered to be suffering from severe poverty.

In Georgia, the subsistence minimum is calculated on the basis of a *consumer basket,* which is not the same thing as a *food basket.* Apart from the essential foodstuffs (thus excluding cigarettes, though they are a part of regular expenditure in most homes), this includes other services and utilities. Since these utilities are shared by all the members of the family, and the costs for each individual cannot be computed separately, the consumer basket is computed for the family as a whole. The basket varies with the size of the family and the age composition of its members.

The same method is used in Mongolia where a total of 508 primary necessary commodities and services are included in the basket. Here eight different types of consumer baskets are constructed for different groups, and the items included in them are valued at current prices. In Bulgaria, a consumer basket is constructed for a family of four since such families are larger in number.

These variations notwithstanding, all the countries included in this project employ the subsistence minimum as the yardstick to measure poverty. There are other measures used by scholars for assessing the extent of poverty in these countries. These are explained below:

Gini Index: This index measures the extent to which the distribution of income, or consumption expenditure, among individuals/households deviates from a perfectly equal distribution. A Lorenz curve plots the cumulative percentages of total income received against the cumulative percentages of recipients, starting with the poorest. The Gini index measures the area between the Lorenz curve and a hypothetical line of absolute equality, expressed as a percentage of the maximum area under the line. Thus, a Gini index of "0" shows perfect equality and an index of 100 represents maximum inequality (see World Bank 1997:261-62).

Decile Coefficient: This compares the average per capita income of the lowest 10 per cent with the average per capita income of the highest 10 per cent of the population. The greater the difference between them, the greater the gap between the rich and the poor. Similar comparisons are also made for the lowest 20 per cent and the highest 20 per cent of the population in terms of income and accumulation of wealth.

Engel Coefficient: This is the ratio of expenditure on food to the family's total general expenses. In 1992, the Russian government set the limit at 68 per cent for households and 83 per cent for pensioners. Households or pensioners spending more than this amount on food were treated as poor. Using this yardstick, the percentage of the poor in 1992 was estimated to be as high as 90.

Poverty Gap: This is used to measure the distance between the poverty line and the mean income of the poor. The formula used for this purpose is:

$$P\,gap = \frac{\sum_{i=1}^{N} (y - x_1)}{N}$$

where y stands for the subsistence minimum, x for the income of the i-th observed household and N for the total number of households observed.

Head Count Index: This is the percentage of people who are below the poverty line. This index does not measure the depth of poverty, however. When the sum of all poverty gaps is multiplied by the head count index, the *Poverty Gap Index is* obtained.

PPP Estimates of GNP per Capita: This is calculated by converting GNP to US dollars on the basis of purchasing power parity rather than the exchange rate. The calculation is made by converting one unit of the currency (the US dollar, in this case) into the number of units of national currency required to buy specific goods and services in another country. The estimates are expressed in international dollars—a unit of account that has the same purchasing power over total GNP as the US dollar (see World Bank 1997: 251).

Country Specificities of Poverty Profiles

We may now briefly review the situation of poverty in the six countries covered by this study.

Hungary

A country of 10.2 million people, Hungary has maintained a -0.3 percent population growth rate since 1980. The country has 7 million people in the age group 15-64, and 71 per cent of them (5 million) are in the labour force---a constant figure between 1980 and 1995. Between 1980 and 1990, the annual growth rate of the labour force was -0.8 per cent; it grew to 0.1 per cent during 1990-95. In 1993, primary school enrolment was as high as 95 per cent for both boys and girls; for the secondary school, the enrolment percentage for boys was lower than girls (79% for boys and 82% for the girls). Only 17 per cent of the children, however, were enrolled in tertiary education. But, what is more important is that no adult illiteracy is reported. The country is also growing more urban: from a 57 per cent urban population in the year 1980 to 65 per cent in 1995. With an average annual growth rate of -1 per cent for the period 1985-95, Hungary's

GNP per capita stood at US $4,120 in 1995, which in PPP terms is around $6,410. Measured in terms of the percentage of people living on $1 a day (PPP), the poor in Hungary constitute only 0.7 per cent of the population according to the World Bank estimates. The average annual inflation rate is 19.9 per cent.

Since the topic of poverty was a taboo during the entire period of socialism, it is difficult to generalise about the growth of this phenomenon; however, several writers are now claiming that it existed during that time. In order to assess post-socialist poverty, Hungarian scholars employ three different approaches. These are: (1) the manifestation of income inequalities; (2) the manifestation of inadequate consumption; and (3) the manifestations of dropping below the minimally acceptable level of living. Using the third approach, Julia Szalai suggests that the ratio of persons living in households with a per capita income below 50 per cent of the average income has been rising since 1992: from 10.1 per cent in 1992, it has gone up to 14 per cent in 1996. There is a high concentration of poverty in the Gypsy ethnic group (66.7%). Szalai also found that poverty is higher in villages (20.1%) than in small towns (13.3%); in the capital city of Budapest, it is the lowest (4.5%). Furthermore, there is a high occurrence of poverty among children: "... low schooling, loss of employment, several small children in the family, and the lack of rural agricultural support to compensate for the decline in cash income result in the frequent occurrence of poverty among young urban families."

Poverty in Hungary is caused by three sets of factors: the uneven socio-economic impact of the economic crisis; the negative consequences of the systemic changes for employment; and the uneven repercussions of prevailing property dealings. The economic crisis is reflected in foreign indebtedness (which is 91% of the yearly gross per capita disposable income---US $1,647 per head in 1995); the rise of consumer prices due to cuts in state subsidies; and the suspension of compulsory employment. In fact, the loss of employment has caused much poverty.

Szalai disagrees with the view that government "overspending" on social benefits and services is the root cause of the problem. She attributes it to the "low efficiency" of the government, which has not been able to develop coherent guidelines for welfare distribution. While "the principles and mechanisms of the socialist way of centrally distributing income" have been suspended in the new regime, no satisfactory alternatives have yet been found. "The still excessive presence of the state in the economy, as well as the understandably open aspiration of its bureaucracy to reinforce its own position of power, persuade the opinion of a broad strata of society against the creation of a private market, which is characterised as a 'foreign' prescription for the process of embourgeoisement in Hungary." The author believes that "the recent expansion of poverty is partly due to the prevailing dogmatic neo-liberal interpretation of a necessary economic transformation, and partly due to those legacies of the state-socialist past which have not yet been terminated." For the eradication of poverty, the author advocates for a wide range of well-targeted interventions, and not just interventions at the macro-economic level resulting in the rise in personal income.

Bulgaria

Bulgaria is classed as a middle-income economy with a GNP per capita of US $1,330, having a PPP value of $4,480 current international dollars. A small country of 8.4 million people, Bulgaria is said to have a poverty level of 2.6 per cent, consisting of those people who live on less than a $1 (PPP) a day. Its population growth has been negative since 1980; for the decade 1980-90, the growth rate was -0.2 per cent, and in the following five years (1990-95), it registered a further decline with an annual growth rate of -0.7 per cent. Its labour force was reduced from 5 million in 1980 to 4 million in 1995. With an insignificant adult illiteracy rate, the country has had a shortfall in school enrolment ratios. In 1993, primary school enrolment was 84 per cent for girls and 87 per cent for boys; at the secondary school level, it was 70 per cent for girls and 66 per cent for boys. Only 23 per cent of the eligible children continued in tertiary education. With a 45.9 per cent rate of inflation, the country is heavily indebted. The net present value of external debt is 87 per cent of the GNP.

Prior to the political changes in 1989, the government did not acknowledge the existence of poverty, although it did refer to people with "low incomes", thus admitting income inequality. The Gini index, computed on the basis of a 1992 survey, stood at 30.8, suggesting an unequal distribution of income. But, even today, "there is no systematic mapping of poverty profiles". Sasha Todorova, the author of the chapter on Bulgaria, holds that various guarantees given to people during the previous regime did succeed in creating satisfactory living standards, but they also contributed to the decadence of society, as people became virtual parasites of the state and lost all motivation to work and earn. When there was a reduction in the protected incomes—salaries, pensions, indemnities, allowances, stipends, etc.—people were rendered poor. Furthermore, a drop in the purchasing power of income affected all citizens. Thus, in Bulgaria, there are people (1) who are "persistently poor", (2) who are in the process of impoverishment, and (3) who could become impoverished in the near future if the same trend continues. It must also be said that different people have different notions of poverty. In a sample survey carried out in 1992 and repeated in 1993, researchers found four different conceptions of poverty among the respondents:

1. incapable of meeting physiological needs (14.1%),
2. incapable of meeting daily needs (23.3%),
3. incapable of meeting physiological and daily needs without state assistance (40.1%), and
4. unable to attain higher living standards (20.6%)

It is logical to collapse the first three sets of responses into a single category and conclude that poverty is defined as the inability to meet basic daily needs. The fourth category is indicative of relative poverty. What the survey data indicate is that while people were able to maintain conventional living standards during communist rule, it has become increasingly difficult to do so now with the withdrawal of state assistance. Bulgarian sociologists, Yossifov and Naoumov, have proposed a four-fold classification of poverty in terms of the behaviour patterns of the poor. They regard these as different sub-cultures of poverty. Based on how the poor themselves perceive and rationalise their poverty, these authors have distinguished between normal, ideological, fatal and pseudo poverty. Normal poverty is defined as income below the average level; ideological poverty is seen as a behavioural norm rejecting social standards and emphasising austere living (as exemplified by hippies, for instance); fatal poverty characterises those who accept their condition as "fate" and resign themselves to it; and pseudo poverty is a synonym for relative poverty, in which people treat the rich as a reference group and regard themselves as poor in comparison. In the absence of any other dependable statistics, the Bulgarian scholars regard as "poor" all those who are entitled to social assistance. This number is much larger than the 2.6 per cent identified by the World Bank as those who are living on less than $1 a day; in fact, their number is constantly rising. Poverty is said to be rampant among the farmers, gypsies, intelligentsia, government employees, ethnic Turks, and those living in the border regions.

Post-communist poverty is said to have been caused by the inefficiency of structural reforms, foreign debt servicing, the high rate of inflation, an ineffective tax policy, and the lack of political consensus. The need to examine employment policy and to consider ways to manage the processes of the informal economy is particularly urgent. Todorova suggests a four-pronged strategy to arrest the growth of poverty: (1) by emphatically speeding up reforms; (2) by improving the social protection of the poorest strata; (3) by taking effective measures to reduce unemployment; and (4) by adequately updating the protected.

Romania

More than double the population of Hungary, and nearly thrice the population of Bulgaria, Romania is inhabited by 22.7 million people, half of whom are in the active labour force---a figure that has remained constant since 1980. The World Bank estimates 17.7 per cent poverty in Romania in terms of the number of those who live on less than $1 (PPP) a day. This datum is significant in view of the fact that the country also has a middle-income economy with a US $1,480 GNP per capita (or a PPP of 4,360 current international dollars)---more or less similar to that of Bulgaria. However, its Gini index (25.5) is lower than Bulgaria's (30.8), which indicates that it has comparatively less income inequality.

Romania also has negligible adult illiteracy and a negative population growth rate (-0.4% per annum during 1990-95). It only has a 12 percent enrolment ratio at the tertiary level, while this ratio at the primary and secondary school levels is more than 80 per cent with little gender difference. Experiencing an annual inflation rate of 68.7 per cent, Romania's external debt is only 18 per cent of the net value of its total GNP (compared to 72% in the case of Hungary and 87% in the case of Bulgaria).

The Romanian government has not been able to arrive at an official definition of poverty. As such, the only poverty prevention measure it has adopted is compensation for the unemployed. It is interesting to note that the 1996 Human Development Report for Romania, prepared by UNDP in collaboration with the National Commission of Statistics, has devoted only a small section to poverty under the heading "Social Equity and Stability: Limiting Social Tensions". The average income of US $86.63 per month certainly indicates poverty. In terms of expenditure, it has been found that an average of 65 per cent of the total household expenses are spent on food, thus leaving only 35 per cent for meeting other basic and social needs. The income gap between the lowest 10 per cent and the highest 10 per cent is constantly increasing—from 6.71 times in 1989 to 8.49 times in 1993. Only 33.6 per cent of households are above the average income level. As opposed to this, 41.5 per cent of households have an income below 60 per cent of the average.

Such a situation is partly attributable to the slower pace of privatisation and marketisation. With the withdrawal of state support and delays in creating a newer system of administration, the growth of the "parallel" or "underground" economy has been encouraged. The privileged strata, including members of the ruling party, have taken advantage of the changing situation and have amassed wealth while the majority have been deprived of the former essential guarantees in the name of liberalisation. State expenditure on social welfare has declined since 1991; in real terms, it is only 77.1 per cent of the 1989 figure, although it constitutes 15.5 per cent of GDP in 1993 compared to 14.1 per cent of GDP in 1989.

In the post-communist regime, there has also been a deterioration of the health services. The government spends only 9 per cent of its budget on medical services, which comes to a meagre 2 per cent of GDP. As a consequence, the people in the medical profession are forced to disregard contractual obligations and cater to the clients who can afford to pay them better consultation fees. The government is also having difficulty compensating the rising number of the unemployed, and providing shelter to the homeless, particularly during the severe winter season.

The growing feeling of relative deprivation, the deteriorating situation of government-supported social services, and the slower pace of economic development in Romania are indicative of the spread of poverty in that country. But, in the absence of dependable data and carefully conducted studies, it is difficult to draw the contours of poverty and to map out appropriate strategies for its eradication. The authors have strongly advocated policy-oriented research. Two preconditions for such research are the training of indigenous social scientists in the methodology of survey research, and the strengthening of social science infrastructures.

Georgia

Inhabited in an area of 70 thousand square kilometres, Georgia has a population of 5.4 million people, which is smaller than the size of Moscow---the capital of the Russian Federation. With a negative growth rate of minus 17 per cent during 1985-95, the country's GNP per capita is US $440 or PPP 1,470 current international dollars. The World Bank Development Report for 1997 does not give any poverty figures (those living on less than $1 PPP a day) for this country, nor does it report its Gini index. The size of Georgia's labour force has held at a constant 3 million since 1980, with a -0.1 per cent growth rate during 1990-95. It has an annual inflation rate of 310 per cent with an external debt of US $1,189 million, constituting 51.6 per cent of the GNP.

An idea of the growing impoverishment in Georgia can be attained from the fact that while during the communist period, as a province of the former Soviet Union, the subsistence minimum constituted only 33 to 40 per cent of the average wage; in the post-Soviet era, the average wage itself has fallen to 37 per cent of the subsistence minimum. Thus, the country draws the poverty line today at the subsistence minimum level (which is the monetary expression of basic minimum consumer goods needed to ensure the normal physiological and social needs of a citizen). Those receiving the average wage are described as suffering from physiological poverty, and those who have no monetary income whatsoever are identified as the absolute poor. However, the government focuses on poverty at the level of the household and not at the level of the individual, which is a very valid premise. Members of a household share common utilities, and therefore the costs for these should be computed at that level and the income of all the members of the family should be aggregated to find out the total resources available to the family. Additionally, Georgia tries to find out whether other resources help maintain the family. For example, households that have access to land and are able to produce food for their own consumption can compensate for a loss in their monetary income.

The informal economy has played a major role as a shock absorber in Georgia. The informal economy here is differentiated from the "shadow" economy; while the latter is somewhat illegal and also criminal, the former is not. Acknowledging the role of the informal economy, and thus hinting at the distorted interpretation of the situation based on official statistics, Avtandil Sulaberidze, the author of the Georgian study, writes: "Even today what baffles people most is the fact that while the formally registered income of many households is ten times less than the survival limit, they are not only surviving but enjoying a reasonably good life." But this observation may not apply to internally displaced persons (IDPs) and refugees who have been severely hit by ethnic conflicts that ensued soon after the birth of the new state. Coupled with the administrative infrastructure's inability to manage the transition to a market economy are the divisive factors within Georgian society that have created a crisis in the nation's cohesion and generated poverty among minority groups. The Georgian population suffers from malnutrition caused by a paucity of food, it lives in poor housing conditions, and it is deprived of adequate transportation and communication. The devastation of the Georgian economic base is attributed by some to the withdrawal of state support; in the Soviet era, this poor region was able to maintain a standard of living similar to other regions through central aid. Now left to its own resources, the country is finding it hard to meet the demands of its population. That is the reason why 71.5 per cent of the urban and 42.7 per cent of the rural respondents in a sample survey identified themselves as poor.

The Russian Federation

The largest of the six countries covered in this study, the Russian Federation is populated by 148.2 million people. Its per capita GNP is also quite high, i.e., US $2,240 or PPP 4,480 current international dollars, higher than Bulgaria, Romania, Georgia and Mongolia, but lower than Hungary. While its primary and secondary school enrolment ratios in 1993 were 107 and 87 per cent respectively, and even tertiary enrollment was as high as 45 per cent, the country has an adult illiteracy rate of 65 per cent according to the 1997 World Bank Development Report. With 84.7 million people in the labour force, constituting 57.2 per cent of the population, only 67.1 million of them were employed in 1995 compared to 75.3 million in 1990, despite the fact that the size of the total population has remained constant during this period. This phenomenon is associated with the growth in the number of workers with two or more jobs. However, having two jobs does not imply having a higher income; those seeking second jobs are the people whose income from their primary job has been declining in recent years, thus causing a need for supplementary income. There is a good deal of hidden unemployment as large numbers of workers have been "laid off". These people are not social misfits, alcoholics or work-shy; they are victims of economic factors of the post-Soviet era that are beyond their control. And they lack the social protection that they would have received had such a situation occurred during the previous regime.

The Gini index of 49.6 (in 1993) suggests that income disparity is growing fast. In that year, the lowest 10 per cent had only a 1.2 per cent share of the total GNP compared to 53.8 per cent amongst the highest 20 per cent, and 38.7 per cent among the highest 10 per cent. Russia's average inflation rate is 148.9 per cent per annum, and the net present value of its external debt is 35 per cent of its GNP.

During the Soviet era, while poverty was officially denied, there was a general acceptance of the fact that about 10 per cent of the people were living below the poverty line. Since the entire Soviet Union pursued the Leninist strategy of the "decommodification of labour", money income constituted only a fraction of the total income of a worker. The money income figures of that era are not an accurate measure of total income. In addition to salaries, people received various other benefits like free services, entitlements and earnings from secondary activities. In the post-Soviet era, labour has been commodified again, and money income is the sole compensation for work in most cases. This is why the country is witnessing massive increases in poverty. There has been a slump in production causing layoffs and non-payment or delayed payment of wages, salaries and state transfers. In addition, the high level of inflation has escalated the prices of all consumer goods.[3] It is said that between 1989 and 1996, the prices of consumer goods have increased by 10,000 per cent. In 1989, the subsistence level was 140 rubles per month for an adult; with inflation, if the same subsistence level were maintained today, it would require as many as 14,00,000 rubles. In present-day Russia, only 10 per cent of the people receive more than a million roubles per month, thereby implying a poverty rate of 90 per cent! With very conservative price escalation figures and a reduction of the consumer basket items, the government has fixed the subsistence minimum at 368,200 rubles or US $55 per month. Against this yardstick, the government has acknowledged the existence of 24.7 per cent poverty. However, those people who have a higher official income on paper, but who are actually receiving much less due to the government's inability to pay salaries in time, must also be figured in this calculation.

In the chapter on the Russian Federation, Pirogov and Pronin have classified low-income people into four categories. At the bottom are the *paupers* whose income is less than the minimum wage; above them are the *destitutes* whose income is less than the cost of the minimum food basket. *Indigence* is experienced by those whose income is less than the official subsistence minimum. Those whose income is above the subsistence minimum but below the social norm for an adequate living standard are described as people with *low provision.* It should be mentioned that the subsistence minimum provides that 61.6 per cent of income goes towards the cost for food for an able-bodied person, and 82.9 per cent for a pensioner. Using this yardstick one finds a striking increase in the incidence of poverty among the "hitherto mainstream groups of society".

According to the 1996 UNDP Human Development Report on Russia, more than half the population had an income less than 150 per cent of the subsistence minimum, indicating that they spent all their income on food alone. They could not even afford to buy a man's jacket as it was 60 per cent of the official monthly subsistence income; in comparison, a woman's spring coat was 127 percent of the subsistence income! With a slump in housing construction, rental prices for houses have gone up and housing scarcity has become quite acute.

What is most striking in the case of Russia is the plight of the intellectual class. Educated and professional workers, and even the military personnel and doctors—all in the employ of the government—have suffered the most. In order to employ more people, the salaries of the already employed have been held down with the result that they receive only 62 per cent of the average wage, and that too is in arrears for long periods of time. During the Soviet era, manual workers and people with mechanical skills were given more weight than intellectuals. And even now there is a continued de-emphasis on their work in relation to technical and specialist skills. This has prompted people from academia to flee the country in search of better job opportunities and higher salaries. Such a flight has obviously generated frustration among less fortunate people who cannot leave the country and are not adequately paid for their services

Mongolia

Of the six countries covered in this study, Mongolia is the smallest in terms of population (2.5 million), and it is not a part of the Eastern Europe. But as an important satellite of the former Soviet Union, and as a Far Eastern country in the process of transition, the Mongolian case is of special interest. It is the country with the lowest GNP per capita at US $310 or PPP 1,950 current international dollars. It has a negative growth rate of minus 3.8 per cent per annum. With an annual population growth rate of 2.1 per cent, Mongolia has one million people in the age bracket 15-64. This is the same size as the country's labour force, of which 46 per cent are female. Although recent statistics on school enrolment are not available, Mongolia had 107 per cent primary school enrolment and 91 per cent secondary school enrolment as early as 1980, suggesting a virtual absence of adult illiteracy in the country. The country is quickly becoming urbanised; from 52 per cent in 1980, its urban population has reached 60 per cent in 1995. Its external debt of US $512 million equals 61.5 per cent of its GNP. The country has an average annual inflation rate of around 51.6 per cent.

Government estimates indicate that poverty has surfaced in the post-communist era. A total of 828,000 people---478,000 from urban and 350,000 from rural areas---are identified as poor, constituting 36.3 per cent of the total population. These people belong to 100,000 households, 43.2 per cent of which are in the capital city of Ulan Bator alone. While the size of the labour force is enlarging there is no corresponding increase in the number of jobs. In December 1996, as many as 55,200 people registered with the labour bureaus as unemployed and looking for work. But, the actual number of the unemployed is hard to guess. There are many unemployed who work in the informal sector, and there are many who do not have jobs but have not registered with the labour bureaus.

Mongolia faces the acute problem of street children who have left their families because of poverty or conflicts with their parents. Efforts to send them back to their families or to rehabilitate them at special centres created especially for them have not succeeded so far because they have been able to earn enough money on the streets to survive and even to support their parents clandestinely. With the halting growth of the private sector, inadequate legislation and deficiencies in administration, people are trying to improve their living conditions in several ways. Some even feel nostalgia for the previous regime in which the state provided support to all, irrespective of their qualifications or productivity. Critics attribute lethargy of the people to the previous system, which made them parasites and quashed their motivation. The competitive character of the market economy makes demands for which neither the government nor the people are fully prepared.

Concluding Observations

The decision to abandon socialism and central planning, and to embark upon the process of transition to a market economy and a democratic form of government has been a mixed blessing for the former socialist countries, now known as countries-in-transition. Suffering for years under totalitarian regimes, the people of these countries saw a ray of hope in the transition: better living conditions, greater freedoms and an invigoration of the stagnating economy. But, the very process of transition caused shock and suffering. The rush to abandon prevailing practices in an almost revolutionary fashion did not allow the administration sufficient time to retool itself, and the exigencies of the emerging situation led it to take ad hoc measures. In the process, it was completely forgotten that changes created by a given social sub-system or cultural pattern have repercussions in the rest of the system. Not prepared to handle the unanticipated consequences—both functional and dysfunctional—the administrative systems in these countries are undergoing a period of stress. The people themselves are ambivalent about the changed situation. The sudden loss of a stable support system and the uncertainty of the future have extinguished their euphoria.

Societies that once claimed egalitarianism and full employment began to reveal their poverty profiles and felt the pangs of the swelling ranks of the unemployed. Contrary to expectations, the transition to a market economy resulted in a loss of jobs and sharp declines in industrial output. Economic collapse, coupled with civil unrest, has caused the escalation of poverty. Barring Poland (where growth resumed in 1992) and Hungary (where poverty could be relatively contained), all other countries of this region recorded steep increases in poverty. Some estimates indicate that between 1989 and 1994, as many as 75 million people fell into the poverty trap in Central and Eastern Europe. In Bulgaria and Romania poverty increased from 1.5 per cent in 1989 to around 27-35 per cent in 1994. Added to this are those who have a "low income", i.e., those receiving 40 to 45 per cent of the average income. The poor are those who receive 60 per cent of the low income.

The following table compares the growth of poverty in Hungary, Bulgaria and Romania:

Table 3

Growth of Poverty in Hungary, Bulgaria and Romania

(in percentages)

Year	*Hungary*		*Bulgaria*		*Romania*	
	Low income	*Poor*	*Low income*	*Poor*	*Low income*	*Poor*
1989	10.1	1.1	n.a.	n.a.	28.2	7.0
1990	n.a.	n.a.	13.8	2.0	21.8	3.5
1991	15.6	2.3	52.1	12.7	28.7	8.6
1992	n.a.	n.a.	55.5	21.8	46.2	16.4
1993	22.5	4.5	59.4	25.3	59.9	25.3

The situation of the former Soviet bloc countries can be described as a transition from *no-poverty* to *poverty*, and it is in the midst of prevailing and growing poverty that a transition to democratic governance and a market economy has to take place. Whether a successful transition will also mean a transition from the present poverty to no-poverty once again, or to a continuance of poverty, is a difficult question to answer since we know that even countries with market economies and democratic forms of government are not spared the scourge of poverty. For instance, a survey carried out in the countries of the European Union in March 1997 has suggested a surprising high level of poverty there: 57 million people, constituting 17 per cent of the European population, are said to belong to poor households. This itself is a good reminder that mere economic growth, or the pursuit of a market economy with a liberal democratic polity, cannot ensure the absence of poverty. It also serves to remind that the strategy to be worked out for the countries of the European Union cannot be the same as those for the countries-in-transition. The root causes of poverty in the two settings are very different.

In the case of the former socialist states, it is hard to generalise about poverty's recent emergence as no data regarding poverty during the socialist times exist. Moreover, the official statistics now available are deficient in many ways and cannot be fully relied upon. Neither the exact number of the poor nor their socio-economic background is known. Responses to poverty have also been different. And, there is an additional point to be made: the recognition of the existence of poverty implies that there are also those who are non-poor—in other words, a stratification that is supposed to be non-existent in an "egalitarian" society has emerged. This could be the reason that when a protest was organised in Russia in March 1997 against unpaid wages, there was a poor turnout. Reporting on this event, the *International Herald Tribune* (28 March 1997) described the behaviour of the non-poor in these terms:

> ... 20 yards from the crowd's rear fringe, under the watchful gaze of Lenin's statue, bustling shoppers in the packed central food market couldn't have been less interested. They were too

busy inspecting pyramids of fresh sausage, glistening racks of fish and a cornucopia of cans, jars and bottles that might have caused a riot in Soviet times.

Quoting from a new survey conducted by the Russian Market Research Company among 4,000 respondents, the Paper said that "average household incomes, officially listed at $120 or so, are in fact at least 70 per cent higher. Even the government has acknowledged its statistics may understate real incomes by a quarter or more."

Poverty in the context of the countries-in-transition has a different face than in other regions. During the socialist era, the countries themselves may have been poor in terms of their GDP or natural resource base, but their societies were characterised by a virtual absence of income inequality. The collapse of that system has generated income inequality in several ways: loss of jobs has caused a loss of income; differential payment for skills has now resulted in income stratification; the liquidation of wealth---through the sale of goods, land, and other hoards, even hidden stacks of foreign currency---by those who had a privileged position in the previous regime has made some richer; and wage arrears have impacted the salaried class and the pensioners. In such a situation, a moneymetric measure for poverty seems to be the only dependable measure. What is interesting is that the concepts of subsistence minimum and food basket that were evolved in socialist times continue to be relevant today, although in a different way. In previous times, computations of the subsistence minimum and food basket were made to fix salaries and wages to ensure that everyone was able to meet his or her basic and social needs. The same measures are used today to determine the gap between the income received and the money needed for the subsistence minimum. While the subsistence minimum was previously lower than the minimum wage, in the changed circumstances it is the minimum wage which has dropped below the subsistence minimum level, making it impossible for a growing number of families to provide for the satisfaction of their basic needs.

What has become clear in all cases is that, while during the socialist regime the costs of the subsistence minimum were lower than the minimum wage, the situation in the transition period has been reversed. Due to inflation, even the average income has become insufficient to meet the needs of the subsistence minimum. The local currencies of all these countries are sliding down on the purchasing power parity index. For example, the Russian ruble, which was more than the value of a US dollar in the 1980s has been devalued so much that today a US dollar can buy as many as 6,900 rubles! It is the same story for other currencies. In 1990, just 2.97 Bulgarian leva could buy a US dollar: today one needs 1,800 leva for the same transaction.

It is also important to emphasise that, unlike in the countries of the "Third World,"[4] in the countries-in-transition poverty has impacted those who are actually employed. The new poor in these countries, whose number is burgeoning, are neither all unemployed nor all illiterate---two characteristics often associated with poverty. Such a profile challenges the common theories on poverty which lead to the cherished prescriptions: educate the poor, generate employment. The poor in these countries are educated---in fact, poverty is greater among those who are more educated, and they are employed. Fostering education and employment do not seem to be the solutions to poverty. Something else has to be done. This is not to deny the importance of education. It would be wrong to say that they are poor because they are educated. The findings from these countries simply challenge the imputed linkage between poverty and education, between poverty and unemployment, and between education and unemployment. These relationships can no longer be taken for granted.

While accepting the importance of education, we are called upon to ponder the kind of education needed in these countries to help them overcome the poverty syndrome. The high enrolment ratios at the primary and secondary schools in all these countries indicate that intervention at that level—in terms of increasing the ratio—is not needed because access to schools already exists. What is perhaps needed is to ensure that these ratios do not drop in the future because of poverty. Secondly, there may be a need to closely examine the content of the curricula and redesign them to meet the new exigencies. Re-education and re-training of the adult population in the new skills needed to operate modern factories, or new office technologies, is another major challenge for education. Initiation of the social scientists from these countries into the methodology of empirical research and the theories of management and administration is yet another aspect to tackle.

On the employment front, actions are perhaps needed both for the creation of new jobs to accommodate youth in search of their first employment, and for the creation of better working conditions for those who are already employed. Here it may be noted that the relationship between employment and a person's well-being is not disputed. However, the evidence from these countries invites us to rethink this association. Generally, poverty is associated with unemployment: people who remain unemployed for longer periods are bound to become poor, and the poor are those who are jobless. In the countries studied here, a new pattern is found. The employed people are also growing poor during the period of transition—whether such a phenomenon is transitional or not is a matter of speculation. Transition to a market economy has changed the employment scenario completely. Previously, the government was the sole employer and pledged to provide full employment to all; now this responsibility is shared by both the government and the private sector. Having ceded most of the units of production to private entrepreneurs, the government's only remaining source of revenue is taxation, and the number of state employees has been drastically reduced. This has resulted in employee layoffs and delays in the payment of salaries on the part of the government; additionally, the financial departments of the government have managed to protect the salaries of their staff and have ignored the claims of other non-financial departments and ministries. Those who lost their jobs in government were not all able to get jobs in the private sector because of changing demands for skills. In such a situation, governments have the responsibility to not only find jobs for those who are seeking employment for the first time; they also have to "relocate" those who have lost their jobs, either through early retirement, or because they were laid off (on one pretext or another). In addition, there is the problem of those employees whose salaries have not been adjusted to rising inflation; they have suffered because of arrears in the payment of their salaries.

The new situation has changed the very structure of the employment market. There has been a massive transfer of employees from the government-run enterprises to the private sector. A serious mismatch between demands for skills and the availability of skills has occurred. The private sector cannot afford the luxury of paying for unwanted skills, or for "slow" and "lazy" workers. Improved coordination between the government and the private sector is needed to protect the interests of employees and to develop a better labour policy. A new relationship will have to be forged between the education system and the world of work to ensure fuller employment and increased productivity. The sudden transition has created a hiatus and jeopardised the interest of the employees.

Pension reforms are equally necessary. Some countries, such as Hungary and Romania, have taken steps to gradually increase the retirement age. Another concern is to protect the minimum pension levels so that pensioners are able to meet the requirements of the subsistence minimum.

The role of the informal sector in the countries-in-transition also needs careful review. Some authors have distinguished between the "black" or "underground" economy and the informal sector. The role played by the informal sector in providing relief to those hit by the transition and the resulting loss of income has generally been appreciated. It is, in fact, viewed as the hidden capacity of the societies to respond to the crisis and provide protection for its members (a virtual safety net). In its absence, there would have been a total chaos, a collapse. Such cultural homeostasis, as revealed by these countries, needs to be documented with carefully planned and executed case studies so that the process can be properly understood and institutionalised. At the same time, there is room to examine the way in which underground economies operate both nationally and internationally.

These cases also invite a careful examination of the newly proposed paradigms of development. The emerging consensus on the failure of the previous paradigms---the modernisation paradigm of the West and the socialist paradigm of the East---taught us that methods of promoting development through state intervention have varied from culture to culture, and that the homogenisation model has been rejected by all.[5] A new development paradigm cannot, therefore, be yet another variant of the homogenisation recipe. The new formula that is now gaining international currency, referred to by some as the "Washington Consensus", suggests a mix of liberal capitalism, democratic polity and good governance. As it is presented, it also seems to be a single recipe for all situations. If the past is any guide, one would doubt its universal applicability. Already, the evidence of these country case studies challenges the idea that this formula can be replicated in the context of former socialist countries. If we looked at the developing countries, we would find at least three different patterns: (1) the "tiger" model—represented by the Republic of Korea, Taiwan, and Singapore—suggests the pursuit of liberal economic growth with an authoritarian rule; (2) the "democratic" model, as in India, where democracy was introduced without waiting for economic development, and the economy is now being liberalised after four decades and a half of successful democratic rule; and (3) the "transitional" model of the East European countries, which have given up both centralised planning and totalitarian regime in favour of a liberal market orientation and a democratic form of government. All three sets of countries are now engulfed in the process of economic globalisation, but the polities in all of them have distinctive features. They may all be called democracies, but they do not correspond to any single model of democracy; and their economies are also responding differently to the global trends. The experiences of all the three sets of countries have been widely different, and all seem to challenge the applicability of a common prescription.

For the countries-in-transition, there cannot be a single prescription as their problem profiles in the present state of transition are vastly different, notwithstanding a common ideological past. The countries-in-transition offer us an opportunity to "take a positive step towards constructing explanations of diversity in the outcomes of liberalization and democratization processes" (Gills and Philip 1996: 589).

Whether simultaneous liberalisation of economy and polity leads to more stability and prosperity, or produces both economic and political destabilisation, is a question that remains unanswered. "Though Chile, for example, seemingly represents a successful model of undertaking both strategies simultaneously and remaining stable and prosperous, it is nevertheless questionable to what extent Chile's economic structure is truly comparable to the advanced industrial economies of East Asia" (ibid) or to the former socialist states covered in this study. "It is... because of the historicity of national development and because cultural and regionally specific factors remain very important, perhaps even central, that diverse patterns of development trajectory will continue to emerge. Particular localities, particular countries, and particular regions will continue to evolve and develop in particular ways..." (ibid).

From the studies on six countries of the former Soviet bloc an idea can be had of the poverty crisis. But, the evidence is not sufficient to suggest concrete actions to remedy the situation. Piecemeal solutions to immediately respond to a pressing need may be helpful in the shorter run, but cannot become part of an overall strategy without properly investigating their repercussions in the wider social system. Similarly, borrowed solutions may not work; what may have been an ideal strategy in a given country may simply be inappropriate in another context because of baseline differences. What is needed, therefore, is a programme of research to study various facets of poverty in different regions and different population groups. Careful analyses of existing policies and the evaluation of programmes of social assistance are a *sine qua non* for developing a proper policy and a plan for the eradication of poverty.

The analysis presented in this book is just the beginning. It provides a good base on which to mount full-length empirical surveys that go beyond the analyses of secondary data. And, the time for this is now.

Notes

1. Replying to a question on the non-inclusion of the industrialised countries on the Human Poverty Index, Richard Jolly, Principal Coordinator of UNDP's 1997 Human Development Report, said: "The measures are not the same. For instance, illiteracy is very low in most industrialised countries. We experimented behind the scenes on some measures such as people who didn't complete secondary schooling, lack of access to water and health services, and unemployment as another indicator. But we thought we would muddle the statistics" (see *Social Development Review* 1997, vol. 1, no. 4:8).
2. For example, the United Nations *Report on the World Social Situation 1993* writes this about poverty: "Some 1,100 million people in developing countries—one in every five people in the world—lived in poverty in 1985. Some three-quarters of the poor, i.e., 57 per cent of the world population, live in South Asia and East Asia. Sub-Saharan Africa has the second largest number living in poverty; 50 per cent are below the poverty line. In West Asia, North Africa, and the developing countries of Europe, 60 million, almost one out of three, live in poverty. In Latin America and the Caribbean, poverty affects about 20 per cent of the population, some 75 million people" (pp.90-9 1). While there is no certainty about the exact number of the poor, as definitions differ, it is generally believed that today 1.5 billion people (out of a total world population of 5.7 billion people) are desperately poor, surviving on a daily income of less than US $1. In 1960, the ratio between the richest 20 per cent and the poorest 20 per cent of the world's population was 30:1, which doubled in thirty years, standing at 61:1 in 1991. These figures give us an idea of the magnitude of the problem.
3. A US dollar today can buy as many as 6,900 rubles; in the 1980s, a ruble was worth more than a dollar.
4. This euphemism has now lost its meaning with the collapse of the so-called Second World. And one is not certain where to

place the countries-in-transition, in the First or the Third World, or to keep them in a world of their own.

5. I made this point in one of my earlier essays thus: "the phenomenon of cultural continuity has challenged the *homogenisation* hypothesis. While individual cultures are experiencing vast changes, they are not becoming similar, not even look-alike. Even their own homogeneity has suffered; they are becoming heterogeneous both in terms of their demographic composition and cultural constitution. The so-called World Culture's monocultural stance is no longer tenable. The plausible perspective is to view both culture and future in their plurality. No single future can be imposed on all cultures" (Atal 1993: 21).

References

Atal, Yogesh. 1971. "The Role of Values and Institutions." In *The Challenge of Poverty in India,* ed. A.J. Fonseca. Delhi: Vikas Publications.

— 1993. "Asian Cultures: What Destination?" In *The Futures of Asian Cultures,* ed. Eleonora B. Masini and Yogesh Atal. RUSHSAP Series # 38. Bangkok: UNESCO.

Atal, Yogesh, ed. 1997. *Perspectives on Educating the Poor.* New Delhi: Abhinav Publications.

Atal, Yogesh and Else Øyen, eds. 1997. *Poverty and Participation in Civil Society.* New Delhi: Abhinav Publications; Paris: UNESCO.

Gills, Barry and George Philip. 1996. "Editorial. Towards Convergence in Development Policy? Challenging the 'Washington Consensus' and Restoring the Historicity of Divergent Development Trajectories." *Third World Quarterly* 17, no. 4: 585-91.

McAuley, Alastair. 1996. "Russia and the Baltics: Poverty and Poverty Research in a Changing World." In *Poverty: A Global Review—Handbook on International Poverty Research,* ed. Else Øyen, S.M. Miller, and Abdus Samad. Paris: UNESCO.

Milanovic, Branko. n.d. *Poverty, Inequality, and Social Policy in Transition Economies*. Washington, D.C.: The World Bank.

Øyen, Else, S.M. Miller and Syed Abdus Samad, eds. 1996. *Poverty: A Global Review—Handbook on International Poverty Research* Paris: UNESCO.

Szalai, Julia. 1990. "Some Thoughts on Poverty and the Concept of Subsistence Minimum." In *Social Report, 1990,* ed. Rudolf Andorka, Tamas Kolosi, and Gyorgy Vukovich. Budapest: TARKI, 296-304.

Tabatabai, Hamid. 1996. *Statistics on Poverty and Income Distribution - An ILO Compendium of Data*. Geneva: ILO.

UNDP. 1996a. *Human Development Report—Bulgaria.*

—. 1996b. *Human Development Report—Georgia.*

—. 1996c. *Human Development Report*—Russian federation.

—. 1997. *Human Development Report—1997.* New York: Oxford University Press.

UNICEF. 1995. *Poverty, Children, and Policy: Responses for a Brighter Future.* Economies in Transition Studies. Regional Monitoring Report No. 3. Florence: UNICEF International Child Development Centre.

United Nations. 1993. *Report on the World Social Situation 1993.* New York.

The World Bank. 1997. *World Development Report 1997.*

3

Education for the Poor and against Poverty

Indian Institute of Education (IIE) organised in 1993 a Series of memorial lectures on Poverty and Education in honour of its founding director, Professor R.V. Parulekar. These were delivered by three prominent social scientists of the country: Y.B. Damle---a sociologist, Durganand Sinha---a psychologist, and N.R. Inamdar---a political scientist. The three scholars examined the relationship between poverty and education from the vantage points of their respective disciplines---sociology, psychology and political science---focusing thus on the non-economic parameters of poverty---a phenomenon which is generally couched in economic terms.

Although I did not have the honour to deliver any of these lectures, or even the privilege of listening to them when they were delivered, I was approached by Professor Chitra Naik (chairperson of the IIE Board of Trustees) to edit them for this book and also to contribute this introductory essay. I could not

---

Written as an "Introduction" to *Perspectives on Educating the Poor* (ed. Yogesh Atal), Abhinav Publications, New Delhi, 1997.

refuse the offer coming as it did almost as a "command" from Chitra Tai whom I hold in high esteem. The offer also came at a right time when the United Nations inaugurated the International Year for the Eradication of Poverty (IYEP-1996) and UNESCO appointed me to "coordinate" the contribution of the Organization to the Year, as well as to the Decade that will be dedicated for this task.

Looking back, it appears very imaginative on the part of the IIE to have chosen this theme in 1993 itself for this series of lectures. It may be recalled that for the World Summit for Social Development that was held in Copenhagen in March 1995, the international community chose "poverty" as one of the three main issues for discussion by the Summit leaders. Thus, throughout the World Summit preparatory process that began towards the end of 1992, poverty-related issues engaged the attention of governments, the scholarly community, and the non-governmental organisations worldwide. Through these three lectures, the IIE has also contributed to this process; it is only proper to have these lectures published for wider dissemination to generate further debate and discussion.

The theme of these lectures is also appropriate as a tribute to Professor R.V. Parulekar (1886-1961) in whose memory they were delivered. A village boy of poor parentage, Parulekar received his early education through support from his relatively well-off kinsmen. His outstanding performance at the matriculation examination earned him a scholarship to join Elphinstone College in Bombay. In addition to a scholarship grant, Parulekar raised his resources by giving "tuition" to other students, and by teaching Sanskrit to interested Europeans. He studied chemistry for his Master's degree, and also did a diploma in Teacher Education. With these qualifications, he became Head Master in a secondary school in his home district of Ratnagiri.

But his return to Ratnagiri was only a brief sojourn, almost preparatory to his departure for higher studies in Britain. Again, he got scholarship to do his M.Ed. degree at Leeds University. It is during his stay in the United Kingdom that he had a chance to listen to Mahatma Gandhi on India's long tradition of learning. Gandhi's speech in 1931 changed Parulekar's orientation to education and made him research old educational records and contribute articles to the Journal named *Progress of Education.* Convinced that the British system of education was incompatible with the needs of Indian society, Parulekar felt uncomfortable as a member of the Government appointed Committee to reorganise primary and secondary education in the then Bombay Presidency, and he decided to opt out of it. This gave him the freedom to articulate his ideas for the expansion of appropriate primary education. His book, *Mass Education in India,* published in 1934, attracted wide attention: *The Times of India*, *Bombay Chronicle*, the *Free Press Journal*, the Bombay Sentinel and several newspapers in Marathi and Gujarati commented favourably on the book in their editorials. His other book, *Literacy in India* (1939), was similarly received by the media and the intelligentsia but it greatly annoyed the government because of the critical assessment he made of the English system of education. The British Director of Public Instruction in the Bombay Presidency thought these books fit to be dumped into the Arabian Sea!!

Parulekar was not only a nationalist; he was a man with ideas. All his life he struggled to eliminate illiteracy, and to Indianise modern education. When the IIE was set up in 1948, its first directorship naturally went to him; he continued on this post until he retired in 1956, at the age of seventy. But he continued to guide research students till his death on October 14, 1961.

Parulekar's interest in education was not just pedagogic. His opposition to the British system of education was also not narrowly political. Although a nationalist, and a follower of

Gandhi, Parulekar introduced a sociological perspective to education by talking in terms of the "needs" of Indian pupils, and the relevance of the curricula. Without using sociological jargon, he drew attention to the interface between education and society and felt strongly that in order to promote literacy in all sections of society, it is important that education is related to the real needs of the people.

Such a position will not be contested today, but the mighty empire of those times continued to pursue its own policy, and established an irreversible trend of western education in the country which is followed even today.

Parulekar's concerns of 1930s are still relevant. Nearly five decades of development in independent India have neither succeeded in eliminating illiteracy, nor in eradicating poverty. Since there is an assumed association between education and poverty, educational interventions have been important elements of most anti-poverty programmes. This must have been the reason behind the decision of the Indian Institute of Education to invite three specialists from different, social science disciplines to speak on the topic of "Poverty and Education". Interestingly enough, all the three speakers accepted the "value" of education and discussed the problems relative to extending education among the poorer strata of Indian society. They approached the problem of poverty from the angle of education, believing that educating the poor is the same as eradicating poverty. In doing so, they ended up talking about education *for* the poor but missed to elaborate how education would work *against* poverty. It is true that India suffers from the twin problems of illiteracy and poverty and efforts are needed to eliminate both of them, but eradication of one does not guarantee disappearance of the other.

Despite nearly five decades of development planning in independent India, the country is still one of the nine giants in the world where there is heavy concentration of illiteracy, and a higher incidence of poverty. From about 16 per cent at the time of independence in 1947, the literacy rate has certainly jumped to an impressive 52 per cent in 1991. But the other side of the coin is that 48 per cent of India's adult population is still illiterate. Such a percentage is not a small number in a country of nearly 900 million: with higher percentage (60.1) of adult illiterates in 1980, this number was 250 million; a 12 per cent reduction in the illiteracy rate in 1995, however, has not stopped the rising number of illiterates that stands at 290 million, 63 per cent of which are women.[1]

In the National Report prepared by the Government of India for the World Summit for Social Development, it is indicated that by the year 2006-07 a 100 per cent literacy rate will be achieved for the age group 15-35 years; but for the age group 7 years and above (that is, including also those who are between 7 and 15, and those who are 35 and above), the target is fixed at 90 per cent, as the following table shows:

Literacy Rate in India (%)

Year	*7 years and above*	*15-35 years*
1980-81	41.4	40.8
1991-92	52.0	56.0
1996-97	75.0	90.0
2006-07	90.0	100.0

Achieving 100 per cent literacy among the people of the age group 15-35 years in the entire country means changing the literacy status of about 110 million people. This figure is, it must be said, an addition to the number of children of the school-going age for whom schooling is to be provided to attain the goal of universal primary education.

The National Report associated the problem of education to population growth and "lack of development in the rural areas, iniquitous distribution of assets in terms of land and water supply in a given rural community and educational deprivation of women" (p. 42). It has also highlighted the need for assigning priority to the education of tribal children. An easy inference can be drawn from the above that the problem of education—understood as spread of literacy and universalisation of primary education—deserves priority attention in the rural and tribal areas, and among women. And since poverty is associated with these segments of society, an educational intervention is expected to contribute to the anti-poverty strategy. The Report clearly states:

> There are certain elements of development which are fundamental to poverty eradication. These are: (i) agriculture and rural development, (ii) food and nutrition security, (iii) literacy and education, (iv) labour-intensive industrialization, and (v) focus on the socio-economically disadvantaged, particularly women and children... (p.20).

Let us compare these figures with the poverty figures. While it is easy to enumerate illiterates, it is difficult to identify the poor. Besides the economic definition of poverty expressed in terms of personal income, poverty is also defined in terms of non-economic indicators: biological or physiological deficiencies, oppression, subordinate position in power structure, unemployment, lack of education, or low standard of living. It is suggested that the greater the number of these indicators present, the higher is the visibility of poverty. But taken any single indicator, as will be shown below, any person's, or group's, identity as poor cannot be determined. In the ultimate analysis, the combined effect of all of these indicators is expressed in moneymetric terms. This is how *absolute* poverty is defined in terms of poverty line which is drawn on the basis of minimum money needed to meet the basic needs---calorie intake, housing, clothing, etc. "The poverty line is", to quote John Friedman, "intended to separate those who fall below it---the *absolutely* poor---from the *relatively* poor who are measured in relation to the incomes of the rest of the society...This second term also suggests the political relevance of income inequality in the economy and may suggest income redistribution policies rather than direct interventions, as in the case of the absolutely poor."[2] I agree with Friedman that "the selection of *poverty line* by distinguishing those who are declared to be poor from those who are not is essentially a political act. Shifting the poverty line up or down by a few dollars can have major implications for the number of people included in each category and on their eligibility for certain kinds of public assistance."[3] Identification of the poor on the basis of poverty line is bureaucratically convenient and politically expedient as public assistance measures can be directed towards the amelioration of their situation and pulling them out of the poverty line. The important point that Friedman has made is that while the approach for the *absolutely* poor is welfarist---just another name for charity---the strategies for the reduction of *relative* poverty require shift in policy in regard to income redistribution. Extension of education for the poor is part of the social welfare approach for the absolutely poor. It is aimed at providing an access to school and to other forms of learning to those who are denied because of poverty. The implicit assumption being that had these people not been poor they would not have remained illiterate (an assumption that needs to be verified) and that they would have sent their children to school

In the National Report submitted by the Government of India to the World Summit for Social Development, "poverty line was adopted as Rs. 20 per capita per month for rural areas and Rs. 25 per capita per month for urban areas at 1960-61 prices. Based on the quinquennial surveys of household consumption expenditure, carried out by the National Sample Survey, the Report has suggested that in 1987-88, the percentage of people below the poverty line was 29.9 (33.4% for rural and 20.1% for urban areas). The latest economic survey (released in January 1996) has brought down this figure for 1993-94 to 19 per cent."[4] Quite understandably, such a low figure raised eyebrows and scholars even questioned the methodology used to arrive at this figure. One economist, S.P. Gupta, used an alternative methodology and computed a figure of 39 per cent which is even higher by 10 percentage points from the official 1987-88 figure.

From the point of view of the relationship between poverty and education, the most striking feature that emerges from the two sets of data—on education and on poverty— is the great disparity between the two: people below the poverty line are smaller in number (whatever estimation we rely on—19% or 39.1% for 1993-94) compared to 48 per cent adult illiterates. Even if we assumed that all those who are below the poverty line are illiterates, we will still find a significant percentage of those who do not qualify to be "absolute poor" but who are illiterate. What, then, is the relationship between poverty and education?

This question can logically be broken into two interrelated questions: (i) what effects does poverty have on education? and (ii) what effects does education have on poverty? In examining this rather complex relationship, it is further necessary to identify the various levels and forms of poverty and the various levels and forms of education. As regards education, the levels are well recognised. Moreover, education is an attribute of an individual; its aggregation at the family or higher levels of social organisation only suggests the total number of people at different levels of education in various social groupings. Like income, education cannot be averaged out. When a person earns, that is income of the family and its per capita value for all the members of the family can be computed, but not so for education.

Poverty, on the other hand, can be conceived at the level of the individual, the family, the community, the region, and the wider nation-society. The criteria employed for defining poverty will differ for each level. Whatever level we may consider, people living in poverty at that particular level do not constitute a single group. From this angle, the broad *categories* of scheduled castes and scheduled tribes do not represent homogeneous population segments. The level of poverty of a tribe in Andhra Pradesh, for example, may be very different from the level of poverty of a tribe, say in Bihar, Orissa or Nagaland. Even in each of these regions, all tribal groups are not similarly poor or rich. The same is true of scheduled castes. Focusing on poverty at the family level, one can find families of identical "poverty-status" in different castes, and a stratification of families within the same caste on a haves-have-nots ladder. Moreover, poverty can be caused by a multiplicity of factors. To quote S.M. Miller: "It can result because many in a group are left behind in deteriorating circumstances as other members emerge, or because a locality's economic opportunities decline. Some are poor because of deliberate policies to repress them economically, politically and/ or socially. Others may be the victims of 'quasi-intentionality' or 'unanticipated anticipatable consequences' where the effects of policy would clearly push people into poverty but no attention was paid to this result."[5] Depending on the source of poverty, the indicator profile also tends to differ from one group of poor to another.

Such a conceptualisation of poverty makes it imperative to evolve culture-specific strategies rather than blindly imitate anti-poverty programmes and strategies that have succeeded in different cultural contexts. It questions the replicability of "best practices" and calls for an empirical grass roots strategy that would work.

It must be admitted that while there are several hypotheses and explanations of poverty, and listings of the "effects" of it, social sciences have not yet come up with a dependable theory of poverty. Apparently looking causal relationships, or plethora of untested hypotheses do not add up to a theory. A complex phenomenon such as poverty cannot be fully understood through narrow lenses of any particular discipline. At the same time, it is also true that planners and policy makers, or even the well-intentioned social workers, could not ceaselessly wait for the arrival of a theory which may follow several large-scale surveys or micro-level case studies. Definition or no definition, poverty and the poor are visible, and their situation is intolerable: if this motivates the civil society and the government to take *band-aid* measures, it is clearly understandable. In a way, such interventions —governmental or otherwise—may be regarded as a means of *ex post facto* testing of a hypothesis, and, thus, as an exercise in applied research.

Quite often, such an exercise mistakes a given characteristic of the poor as the cause of poverty. To be sure, a visible/ noticeable characteristic is an outcome of certain causative factor(s). The fact that many poor in a given sample score zero or low on the scale of literacy cannot *logically* lead to the conclusion that illiteracy is the *cause* of poverty. By the same token, neither can it be said that all illiterate are poor, nor that all poor are illiterate. Some from the non-poor group may be illiterate—for example, mothers and grandmothers of several middle class families in India (a point which is supported by the very low level of female literacy in India even today); similarly, there may be literates among the poor. Folk wisdom in India has always distinguished, for example, between worshippers of Saraswati (goddess of learning) and that of Lakshmi (goddess of wealth); the implication being that scholarship and riches may not go together. In ancient India, the *rishies* were respected for their scholarship; and these were the people who would renounce wealth and all material possessions to lead a life of simplicity and austerity. In a sense, they deliberately chose to live almost near the poverty line! They derived their prestige and esteem from wisdom and not wealth.

To education (i.e., lack of it) as an indicator of poverty status, let us add yet another indicator---unemployment. It is also generally believed that unemployment is the cause of poverty, and education is offered as a means to solve the problem of unemployment. Implied in this formulation is a chain of explanations: illiteracy leads to unemployment, which leads to poverty. From this, it is also derived that the "poor" are unemployed. Accepting this formulation would mean denying the existence of unemployment among the educated, and also of poverty among the employed. We all know that such is not the case. Referring to the relationships between education and income, Blaug says: "After two decades of intensive research on the association between education and national income around the world, little more can be said than that a 10 per cent rate of enrolment in primary schools and a 40 per cent literacy rate is a necessary but, alas, not a sufficient condition for rapid economic advance. It is easier to show that nations are better educated because they are rich than that they are rich because they are better educated."[6] Blaug's researches refute the alleged relationship between illiteracy and unemployment.[7]

Available statistics from the developing countries only suggest some sort of causal relationship between education and employment particularly in the initial phases of educational expansion. Where there is a low percentage of the educated, there is also negligible unemployment among the educated. But as education expands, as is the case in India, there is a transformation of the uneducated unemployed into educated unemployed—a point that supports Blaug's conclusion.

The prevalence of educated unemployed leads one to question the alleged causal relationship between poverty and unemployment. Unemployment statistics from several countries reveal that it tends to be higher among the educated than among the illiterates, and that among the educated, its concentration is to be found in the middle range; the lowly qualified, or very highly qualified, have lower percentage of unemployment than those who are in between these two extreme categories.

Such configuration of unemployment prompts me to suggest that unemployment is basically a middle class phenomenon. The very poor, who struggle for their subsistence, cannot afford the luxury of being unemployed. They would engage in whatever activity that is available for them and earn the living, and they would mobilise the entire human resources of the family in that task. The middle class family, on the other hand, can support an unemployed member of the family during the latter's search for a suitable job. The period of unemployment in such cases is, in effect, *a waiting period* for the first-job seekers.

Researchers in India, for example, have worked out average waiting period for different types of educated job seekers which ranges anywhere between six to eighteen months. In the economies where job security is ensured and, thus, where there is very little by way of inter-organisational occupational mobility, a person's unemployment period ends with the entry into the job. Since that job defines the latter's career, a person willingly suspends the decision to enter a job until a right one is found. Of course, constant frustration in getting the right job may lead one to end the search abruptly and accept whatever is available as a compromise.

This formulation, however, does not suggest that no relationship exists between the variable of poverty and unemployment. In fact, long periods of unemployment, or a sudden loss of job, can create hardship for the person and his family and even lead to their impoverishment; poverty thus created may pose difficulties for the family in providing adequate education to its young for a brighter prospect in future.

Poverty diacriticals may lead to social degradation and loss of esteem. The relationship between these variables, thus, is cyclical; simple cause-effect relationship cannot be established between them. It is important to emphasise the need to see these phenomena in the wider context of the social system in which all parts are affected by, and affect, other parts, directly or vicariously. Thus, the phenomenon of "unemployment", or of "poverty", has to be understood in the socio-cultural context in which it occurs.[8]

It is now widely acknowledged that poverty is a multidimensional phenomenon. It is caused by a variety of factors, in different combinations, and it has a multiplicity of consequences. As such, poverty eradication calls for a holistic approach, in place of the sectoral. A clinical approach, treating the visible symptoms, does not take us to the root of the problem. If, for example, illiteracy is caused by poverty, mere eradication of illiteracy will not eradicate poverty. The fact of the matter is that illiteracy is not "caused" by poverty in the sense that a literate individual falling prey to poverty will not be rendered illiterate. What poverty does to an individual living in poverty is to "disallow" him or her, or to make it difficult for him or her, to become literate: in other words, poverty *perpetuates* illiteracy, it does not undo literacy. Thus, it is necessary to eradicate poverty in order to promote literacy. Focus on removal of illiteracy is, thus, only indirectly connected with the objective of poverty eradication. Irrespective of the poverty profile, literacy drive would change the literacy profile of an individual or group which would, in turn, facilitate social, psychological and geographical mobility of that unit, and prepare it for devising different survival strategies. But literacy changes only one indicator of poverty. Improvement in the literacy profile does not automatically result into decline in the overall poverty level.

It is for this reason that the World Summit for Social Development opted for a broader definition of poverty, and sought for an integrated approach for its alleviation, and for its ultimate eradication. Poverty eradication strategy must attempt to eliminate hunger and malnutrition, provide food security, ensure employment and sustainable livelihoods, increase access to basic services and amenities (health, water, shelter, sanitation and education), and promote participation in political, social and cultural life. Poverty eradication should result in restoration of self-confidence and creation of such mechanisms and processes which will prevent a lapse into poverty.

In any strategy of poverty eradication, education plays an important role. But education alone does not provide the magic wand to eradicate poverty. And education's role has also to be properly defined. I would argue that the role of education should not be seen only vis-a-vis the poor: education of the non-poor is equally important in this context. After all, "it is the culture of the non-poor that keeps the poor in their poverty place. The culture of the non-poor denies economic opportunities to the marginalised..., isolates them socially so that they cannot participate effectively in the larger society, and encourages their political, economic and social exploitation."[9] Apart from changing the mindset of the non-poor relative to the poor and poverty, there is also a need to develop better tools for the investigation of poverty and to establish effective interfaces between the social science researchers, community, and the policy makers and planners.

Education of the poor is not simply a matter of "extending" that education which is provided to the non-poor. Not because we should try to create differentiation between "elite" and "non-elite" education, but because we must judge its acceptability and relevance to the recipient population. Acceptance of a form of education would depend upon the perception of its "relevance" and of its "immediate consequence" by the poor. If education is seen as producer of "unemployed" educated youth, resistance against it cannot be easily dismissed. In our enthusiasm to spread education we sometimes forget this aspect and experience costly failures in terms of high drop-out rate, greater absenteeism and criticism by the community of the irrelevance of education.

There is one additional element of considerable significance relative to education and stratification that is generally not mentioned. In stratification terms, poverty is a reflection of inequality; removal of poverty implies promotion of equality. Granting that no society is free of strata and, therefore, of inequalities, equality is qualified as "equality of opportunity", or "equality of access". Education is seen as a means to attain equailty.

The system of modern education, as it is practised in India, is based on the premise of performance and competition. A pupil's learning is graded in terms of his/her performance at the examination. Students belonging to the same class get, over time, stratified into better and poor performers, and are accordingly either promoted to a higher class, or asked to repeat. Not all those who are promoted secure the same grade; a class of equals in the beginning becomes a class of unequals in the end. Apart from a person's socio-economic background there are several other factors that contribute to this inequality. Given this format of learning, which weeds out non-performers and stratifies performers in different levels of achievement, education can be seen as contributory to the process of stratification. Creation of inequality is, in a way, inherent in the very process of education. Added to this are the accentuating factors that are discussed at great length in Professor Durganand Sinha's paper.[10] How can, then, education create equality? One wonders whether the principle of "equality of opportunity" can be applied at all levels of education without compromising with the very basis of education. There is some merit in the proposition that as far as education is concerned, the principle of equality of opportunity should be applied at the initial point of entry in the education system after which further ascendancy should be governed by the educational process itself. This argument does not imply "denial" of higher education to a meritorious but poor person; it is denial to anyone who does not "qualify" irrespective of one's wealth status. It also asserts the need for developing mechanisms to improve performance of the deficient ones by extending the period of learning, by improving the quality of instruction and of the learning environment, and by channelling students in different streams of their respective choosing. Positive discrimination alone for those who have suffered from negative discrimination in the past may not be the appropriate recipe; it is only going from one extreme to another and, in the process, creating newer victims for negative discrimination. What a society needs to ensure for its social development is to erase all kinds of negative discrimination; selective positive discrimination in favour of one group is just another name for selective negative discrimination against another group. Such an approach cannot break the vicious cycle of discrimination and cannot halt creation of antagonistic groups. It is interesting that V.P. Singh who, as Prime Minister, took the cause of *Dalits* along the lines of Mandal has recently made a remark that supports the observation I am making. He said: "Victims of caste oppression should not create fresh victims along caste lines" (*India Today*, June 30, 1996, p.18—International Edition).

Professor Inamdar's lecture[11] has particularly focused on constitutional provisions, as part of the "Directive Principles" and "Fundamental Rights", meant to positively discriminate in favour of the scheduled castes and scheduled tribes. There was a major study carried out in eighteen states of the Indian Union, under the auspices of the Indian Council of Social Science Research (ICSSR), in the 1970s to evaluate the impact of education among the scheduled castes and scheduled tribes. This mammoth study, in the designing of which I actively participated, was mainly concerned with the question: Why is it that the educational profile of these groups has remained low despite all the efforts by the government and various non-profit organisations? It is a pity that the findings of various regional studies were not synthesised to draw all-India conclusions. However, there was one significant pointer: most of the benefits of these schemes went to the "rich" among the "lower" groups. Although it may be politically disturbing datum, the inference that can be drawn from this is that "poverty" cannot be generalised at the level of caste. Poverty, or economic backwardness, is usually an attribute of the family. Therefore, anti-poverty interventions must be targeted at that level. However, if an entire "local community", which may consist of many castes or ethnic groups, suffers from relative deprivation, strategies appropriate to alleviate that situation must be evolved. But this distinction between the two forms of poverty is important.

Drawing from a variety of psychological researches carried out both in India and abroad, Professor Durganand Sinha's paper[12] tries to explain differential performances of the poor and the non-poor. Psychological researches have mainly focused on the impact on learning of malnutrition, of child socialisation, and personality and motivational dimensions. He has also summarised researches that deal with the school environment, including teacher attribution on the performance of students. In sum, psychological researches suggest that "if proper intervention is made at the appropriate time, the disadvantaged child need not remain in the condition of poverty but can acquire appropriate cognitive, linguistic and other skills to develop out of it."

The three lectures have focused on the question of removing illiteracy and extending primary education. And these efforts are to be targeted among the poor strata of society. They can be regarded as contributory to the process of eradication of poverty. This is to see the problem of poverty from the angle of education. An educational intervention would change the literacy profile of a given group, and may even prepare the younger population for a better job in the future which may take out the family from the vicious circle of poverty. In that sense, education is an investment; its dividends are, however, not immediate. Those who are concerned with the removal of poverty will have to attack on several fronts: providing immediate relief---from hunger, disease, malnutrition, lack of shelter etc.---and creating conditions that would not let them lapse into poverty. They will also have to develop mechanisms by which "poverty" does not recur---and in this, education's contribution is manifold: universal education, special and vocational education, and higher education in all fields to promote both fundamental and applied research so that disasters are anticipated, and precautions are taken in time, and the fruits of advances in science and technology can be enjoyed by all sections of society. There is need to look into curricula and the very system of imparting instruction and judging student performance.

Education alone would not solve the problem of poverty, but poverty cannot be eradicated without education. The question that needs to be continually asked is what kind of education? Its answer should differ from country to country and within a country from region to region. An education that purports to homogenise cultures has lost its appeal; to preserve our creative diversity we need education that respects heterogeneity of cultures, and prepares societies for their respective futures.

Notes

1. According to 2001 census, the literacy rate stands at 65.38 per cent (75.85% for males and 54.16% for females). The number of illiterates is a whooping 461 million, of which women are 268 million (58% of all illiterates).
2. John Friedman, "Rethinking Poverty", *International Social Science Journal,* 148, June 1996, p. 163.
3. Ibid.
4. See *Business India,* March 11-24, 1996, p. 63 and also note that this article mentions 25.3 per cent figure for 1987-88 as against the figure of 29.9 in the official report submitted to the World Summit for Social Development.
5. S.M. Miller, "The Great Chain of Poverty Explanations" in *Poverty: A Global Review* (eds. Else Oyen, S.M. Miller and Syed Abdus Samad), UNESCO, Paris, 1996, p. 585.
6. Mark Blaug, "The Quality of Population in Developing Countries, with particular reference to Education and Training" in *World Population and Development: Challenges and Prospects* (ed. Philip M. Hauser), Syracuse University Press, 1979, p. 364. See also M. Blaug, *An Introduction to the Economics of Education,* London: Penguin, 1970, Chapter 3.
7. See Blaug, op. cit. (1979), p. 368.
8. The remarks on unemployment and education are adapted from a keynote address I delivered at the Fourth Olympiad of the Mind held at Harvard University in May 1994.
9. Miller, op. cit., p. 579.
10. See *Perspectives on Educating the Poor* (ed. Yogesh Atal), Abhinav Publications, New Delhi, 1997.
11. Ibid.
12. Ibid.

4

Involving the Poor: The Many Question Marks

> It is now common to demand that the rich nations convert their war machine into a programme for the development of the Third World. The poorer four-fifth of humanity multiply unchecked while their per capita consumption actually declines. This population expansion and decrease of consumption threaten the industrialised nations, who may still, as a result, convert their defence budgets to the economic pacification of poorer nations. And this in turn could produce irreversible despair, because the plough of the rich can do as much harm as their swords.
>
> —Ivan Illich, *Celebration of Awareness: A Call for Institutional Revolution*, Penguin, 1973:1321

The decision of the United Nations to convene a World Summit for Social Development in Copenhagen in March 1995 brought the social question in prime focus. Through the preparatory process, the Summit mobilised not only the governments, but

---

Reprinted from *Poverty and Participation in Civil Society* (eds. Else Øyen and Yogesh Atal), UNESCO and Abhinav Publications, New Delhi, 1997.

also the NGOs, other inter-governmental organisations---both regional and international—and the scholarly community to think about the prevailing social crises and come up with "do-able" solutions. UNESCO participated in this process and convened a number of seminars on various aspects of social development nationally, regionally, and internationally to catalyse thinking and promoting debate and dialogue on issues related to development. It also supported the work of the Comparative Research Programme on Poverty (CROP)---a research programme initiated by the International Social Science Council. Among others, UNESCO assisted CROP in the organisation of an international symposium in Paris, in December 1994, to discuss the current status of research on poverty in different regions of the world. That exercise helped identify the researched areas and the gaps that exist which need to be filled through priority research. A book based on the updated papers presented at the symposium was recently released by UNESCO under the title, *Poverty: A Global Review—Handbook on International Poverty Research.*

Taking advantage of the Summit, UNESCO sought a slot from the Summit organisers to convene a special Round Table on Participation of the Poor in Civil Society. The Round Table was organised, jointly with CROP, on 7 March 1995 at Eigtvedt Pakhus. It was attended by more than 350 participants including social scientists, politicians, bureaucrats, and the NGOs.

The holding of the Summit was a recognition of the fact that the social crisis has affected not only the countries of the developing world---the so-called South---but also the western world as well as the former communist/socialist countries. Poverty, unemployment, and social disintegration---the three key problems chosen for the Summit deliberations and the Programme of Action---are experienced by all the countries of the world, though their manifestations are different. The search for their solutions, therefore, is universal as the presently prescribed remedies have generally failed everywhere. These three problems are interlinked and, therefore, their solution calls for an approach that goes beyond economism and sectoral perspectives.

It is totally unacceptable that more than one billion people continue to live in poverty. Despite unreliable statistics, no one disputes that a vast humanity suffers from *illth*—ill-fed, ill-clothed, ill-housed, ill-educated or even illiterate, and ill-healthy. But the questions are: How to eradicate poverty? How to ensure that poverty will not recur? Does *wealth* provide an answer to *illth?*

There is an emerging consensus that universal problems do not have universal answers. The paradigm of development that guided the past five decades of development was based on the premise that a single recipe is universally applicable. We all know that the Second World followed the Marxian recipe, and the First World despatched the capitalist recipe to the so-called Third World. What has been the outcome? The Second World collapsed, and the Third World continues to confront the same social crises with greater intensity, and is now joined in this pain by the First World as well.

The end of the cold war era has given a new context to focus on the problem of social development. Already, in the 1970s, a disenchantment with the prevailing paradigm of development had begun and scholars started thinking in terms of alternative approaches. In the countries of the Third World, the rising revolution of aspirations and expectations----that occurred soon after the independence from the erstwhile colonial rules—started fading in the wake of a rising revolution of frustrations. Of course, development did occur, but neither it did bridge the gap between the developed and the developing countries, nor did it uplift the people from the shackles of poverty. Economic development did not lead to social development; transfer of technology did not erase the dark spots of underdevelopment.

In the late 1970s, and in the early 1980s, the international community started talking in terms of "endogenous development". As if this shift in emphasis was not clear, the late 1980s saw the emergence of the new buzzword: "human resource development". Concerns related to environmental deterioration took the leaders of the world to Rio where the new coinage of "sustainable development" received international recognition. The road leading to Copenhagen from Rio in 1995 defined its new destination: "social development". Reaching this destination required overcoming three major hurdles: poverty, unemployment and increasing tendencies towards social disintegration and marginalisation. Fifty years of development experience notwithstanding, poverty is identified as a major social crisis that is inflicting not only the countries of the developing and the least developed world, but also those countries who boasted of being "developed" and who had been exporting their development recipes to the developing countries all these years.

It is known history that the era after the Second World War polarised the First World and the Second World. The leaders of these two 'worlds' tried to woo the Third World that consisted of the decolonised nation-states in Asia and the Pacific, Africa, and in Latin America. Pre-packaged solutions, derived either from the ideology of communism or the "praxis" of capitalism, were offered to the newly independent nations to hasten the pace of their development and become part of the process of globalisation. The countries of the Third World provided experimental playgrounds to the technicians and experts from the developed world. But they did not succeed in transforming these societies into their mould. The old adage that East is East and West is West and that the twins shall never meet remained valid with the replacement of East by the word South, and of West by the word North. The talks of North-South dialogue and of South-South dialogue characterised the international milieu of the 1980s. Definitely, a need to rethink development was felt everywhere. It was in response to this that various world conferences were organised under the auspices of the United Nations and its specialised agencies so that a new Agenda for Development can be drafted.

The Copenhagen Summit on Social Development was an official recognition, at the international level, of the failure of the past efforts to promote social justice through eradication of poverty, provision of sustainable livelihoods, and promotion of social integration. Not only that the dominant paradigm of development failed in the countries where it was imported and imposed, it also did not succeed in promoting social development even in the countries where it had originated. We have thus reached a situation where although the need for development has not died down, but the prevailing recipe for development has been rejected. And there is no replacement in sight.

The need for a new agenda for development can be seen in the context of a changed political scenario, both nationally and internationally. The end of the cold war has changed the rhetoric of international politics. The former communist states are struggling to create new institutions on the ashes of the old; in the process, they are facing new problems. The 1993 Report of the United Nations on the "World Social Situation" acknowledged the fact thus: "Poverty has now come into the open in the economies in transition. A drastic drop in production, a steep rise in prices and the new phenomenon of unemployment have created a class of poor people hitherto absent in economies in transition" (p.xvii). In other parts of the world, there are trends towards transition to democracy. This has opened up new space for discourse and dialogue. There is also recognition of the fact that, like the developed countries, in the developing countries as well, there are other actors that are competing for the roles that were earlier performed only by the state. There is a realisation that while the institution of the state remains an important and indispensable structure in any polity, it is not able to carry out all the tasks by itself. The role of the private sector, and of the non-governmental organisations (NGOs) is equally important as these are defined by some as key components of a "civil society". It can be argued that any agenda of development must recognise the presence of these other actors and that they should be involved in the development effort. The emergence of these structures within a society has also led to a need for the redefinition of the role of the external agents such as other governments, and the international system consisting of inter-governmental organisations and NGOs, as well as multinationals.

The newer emphasis on endogenous development is not a denial of the role of the external forces and agents of change; it is only a rejection of pre-packaged solutions coming from abroad with total disregard of the socio-cultural reality of the recipient society. The international community has learnt the costly lesson that while there are global problems—problems that are faced everywhere—there are no global solutions. "Think globally, act locally" has become a new motto. Global thinking on alternative development has become a new academic style. However, what has emerged, as a result of this change in orientation, is a series of competing models, each of which is presented by its proponents as the alternative to replace the conventional one. While strong criticism is in evidence of a *single* paradigm of development that reigned supreme all these years, scholars still continue to propose single alternatives, as replacement, rather than allowing multiplicity of models that may compete and co-exist. It should be for the societies to select or reject any innovation, or a strategy for development, in terms of their own cultural contexts. As there is a strong support for the maintenance of "biodiversity", so is now an acknowledgement of the importance of "cultural diversity". No development strategy that intends to homogenise cultures can succeed. Societies wish to develop without sacrificing the specificities of their cultures.

It is in such an intellectual atmosphere that one finds some development theorists and practitioners recommending the strategy of participation to correct the wrongs of the past. While this word "participation" is in vogue, different meanings are attributed to it. As an example, one may refer to the 1993 UNDP *Human Development Report*, which begins with the admission: "People's participation is becoming the central issue of our times." It refers to an "impatient urge" among the people "to participate in the events and processes that shape their lives". Referring to the continuing exclusion, the Report highlights the fact that more "than a billion of the world's people still languish in absolute poverty, and the poorest fifth find that the richest fifth enjoy more than 150 times their income". In order to change this unacceptable situation, for which the time appears to be appropriate, the Report has argued a case for the redefinition of many old concepts. It says: "Security should be interpreted as security for people, not security for land. Development must be woven around people, not people around development---and it should empower individuals and groups rather than disempower them. And development cooperation should focus directly on people, not just on nation-states." The new definition of participation offered by the Report seeks for widespread participation in all aspects of development. "Markets need to be reformed to offer everyone access to the benefits they can bring. Governance needs to be decentralised to allow greater access to decision-making. And community organizations need to be allowed to exert growing influence on national and international issues."

There is, thus, a growing opinion that "participation in civil life" is one of the necessary means to overcome the disadvantage of poverty. But, how is participation a key to poverty alleviation? The answer to this question is not simple. There is, first of all, a crisis of definition of both the concepts---that of poverty and of participation. Nobody denies the existence of poverty and of the poor people, and yet there is no consensus on the definition, particularly, on the criteria or indicators to be employed in identifying the poor. A majority regards poverty an economic phenomenon, locating its indicators in material conditions. On this ground, four distinct levels of poverty are identified: destitution, or extreme form of poverty; the ranks of the very poor who have bare minimal level of living; the poor who are marginally above the level of subsistence; and the people with low incomes---the relatively poor. These conditions of poverty can be assessed at the level of the individual, the family, the community, or the nation.

There are also those who regard poverty as a matter of perception. Poverty may become a "way of life", a "culture", and people living that culture may not feel its pinch until they are exposed to other relatively affluent conditions and begin comparing themselves. A contact with the outside world creates a new reference group orientation for the community as a whole which may start regarding itself relatively "inferior" or "superior" vis-à-vis the external reference group. Such poverty perception by the entire community is qualitatively different from the perception of poverty by a family or sub-group within a community in the framework of internal reference groups. As a consequence of colonisation, for example, all colonised societies were treated by the colonial regimes as "primitive", "backward", "underdeveloped"---all these adjectives used as synonyms of poverty in a comparative frame of reference. These characterisations were given by the "outsiders" who clubbed all the "insiders" into a single category.

For the proper identification of a group, the distinction between "self-definition" and "definition-by-others" is very important; where the two definitions correspond, the identity question is easily resolved, but where there is a conflict between the two definitions, the crisis is of a different order. A group defining itself as belonging to the category of the "poor" may not be accepted by the "others" as poor; similarly, any group may resent being called "poor" by those not belonging to it. Of course, when objective criteria of deprivation are used to determine the extreme form of poverty---destitution---the status question might become irrelevant. Since participation has to do with the enhancement of the status, it can be argued that it will have little relevance for the destitutes who are desperate to fulfil their basic, minimal needs.

For handling the problem of poverty, one will, of course, have to go beyond the definitional controversies, and analyse the factors that cause poverty. For example, a tribal community living at a lower stage of economic and technological development requires a different strategy for its poverty alleviation than, say, a community that has been destroyed by an earthquake, or is made to leave its locale because of a war and become a refugee. In other words, there is a difference between *ascribed* poverty and *achieved* poverty. It should be obvious that solutions to these two different kinds of poverty cannot be the same. Even if "participation", for example, is suggested as a remedy, it will be necessary to specify the kind of participation that is needed to come out of a specific type of poverty. The hurdles in the path of poverty elimination differ from one kind of poverty to another and, therefore, there cannot be a single solution to overcome the various types of hurdles. There cannot be a common answer to the problem of poverty in Bosnia, or Cambodia, or Rwanda, notwithstanding the fact that all the three states have suffered from internecine wars. Their location in Eastern Europe, Asia, and Africa respectively, their distinctive demographic composition, the level of their economic and technological development, and the different histories of their political regimes---to name a few differences in them, will have to be taken into account to formulate workable solutions to the problems that confront these societies. We will have to rigorously think in terms of culture-specific strategies.

Several people have hinted at the shortfalls of moneymetric indicators and have argued that the level of "well-being" is an important manifestation of poverty. The indicators to measure well-being are rather more difficult to construct as they will have to accommodate culture-bound definition of well-being and to assess the subjective feelings of the people whose well-being is intended to be measured.

While debate regarding the definition of the poor and of poverty remains unresolved, questions are also raised about the prescription of participation. The theme chosen for the Round Table subtly linked poverty with participation with the subjunctive "and". This relationship can be treated in a variety of ways. One common interpretation is that the poor "do not participate" or are "disallowed to participate". In either case, the implicit assumption is that "participation" is important and if the poor "begin" or are "allowed" to participate, they will have gone the first step towards alleviating their poverty. This assumption calls for serious scientific investigation in different cultural settings and among different kinds of the poor---e.g., poor as an "ascribed" status or an "achieved" status. Such an inquiry will have, similarly, to identify the different kinds of participation---political participation, participation in decision-making outside the home at various levels of administrative hierarchy, participation in economic life, participation in socio-religious life of the community (which may be hampered either because of the lack of resources, or of an ascribed low status that denies participation and inclusion)---and objectively define the "desirability" of participation in a cause-effect relation mode:

hypothesis that X (participation) removes/facilitates in the removal of Y (poverty). Since there could be X_1, X_2, X_3,...X_n, and similarly, there could be Y_1, Y_2, Y_3,...Y_n, the apparently simple looking relationship may, after all, be not so simple. We know that the poor live in a world of multiple realities, and that poverty takes many forms. We also know that the poor cannot afford to remain idle as they have to continuously struggle for their survival. Thus, as an active population, they are continuously participating. What does, then, participation mean really?

It may be worthwhile here to recall the period of the 1950s when the concept of community development was introduced in the developing countries to promote rural development. When people offered resistance to outside innovations, development agents first blamed the traditional cultures for their backwardness and then called for "people's participation". What they meant by such "participation" was the involvement of the people in implementing the "projects" that were designed by outsiders. The priorities assigned by these external agents of change were falsely termed as "felt needs" of the people. Thus, participation in the form of free donation of manual labour, for example, was sought by the development agents. People did not participate in the planning process, nor was their participation sought for that purpose, as all planning was done centrally at higher levels. What the development personnel meant by participation was the "use" of the locally available labour force in the implementation of local projects.

There are other examples of efforts to bring in the poor in the participating arena of the non-poor. In electoral politics, in the countries that have adopted a democratic path, participation of the poor implies their voting behaviour; all political parties try to tap this enormous "vote bank". From this angle, it is very instructive to note that there exists almost an inverse relationship between education and voting. In India, for example, voting in the first general elections was as high as 75 to 80 per cent on an average when country's literacy rate was as low as 16 to 18 per cent; now with the rising literacy rate, the voting percentage is increasingly coming down in successive elections. In contrast to this, in a high literacy country, such as the USA, the polling percentage in the Presidential elections is not even 50. One can, therefore, argue that a deliberate non-participation in a political activity is also a form of participation; similarly, it can be said that blind voting is as good as non-participation. And, the relationship between literacy and voting is not straightforward.

When discussing participation of the poor in civil society one will have also to define the very concept of civil society. Is civil society an opposite of the government? Does the word "NGO" include also the so-called private sector? Are the NGOs not part of the environment of the non-poor? It is well known that many organisations work "on behalf" of the poor, but they are not run by the poor. The spokespersons for the poor are not always the poor; what they represent are their own perceptions of the poor, or of poverty, and their own prescriptions for the elimination of poverty. Such NGOs only "co-opt" and "incorporate" the poor, as the poor neither have the luxury of time or of resources to "waste" in activities that do not directly and immediately benefit them and the members of their family in material terms. Studies in the field of sociology of revolution have suggested that all revolutions are engineered by the leaders who come from the "middle class"—a nebulous concept indeed; they have both the time and the means to think, to articulate demands and ideologies, and to organise protests. The poor do not have time for such "luxuries"! They are "used" by the middle classes and are drawn into the struggle by those who proxy for them; and the struggle is misnomered as "people's struggle". It may be recalled here that most socialist states called themselves "people's democratic republics" when they were, in fact, run by a party caucus and in a non-democratic (authoritarian, totalitarian) way. Labels were the masks to hide the reality.

An answer to the question as to why do people not participate may lie in another question: what would they get out of participation? Participation, by itself, does not directly eliminate poverty. Moreover, participation depends also on the level of skills and knowledge as much as on the motivation. An illiterate who had not been exposed to the wider world can only participate in the world that he/she knows; he/she cannot become a regional or a national planner because his/her cognitive horizons are not that vast, and because he/she does not possess competence in macro-economics. The higher the level of decision-making, the higher are the demands of competence and specialisation. It appears that when participation is discussed, only the community level is taken into consideration. Even at that level, as also at higher levels, denial of participation may not always be based on the criterion of poverty. There are different domains of decision-making and each domain has its own peculiarities that determine the type and extent of participation by different actors. Is it not more than a cliche to suggest that "top-down" planning be replaced by "bottom-top" planning? If there is a need to do something at the bottom—the grass roots---there is also a need to do so at the top. One-way traffic from the bottom makes as little sense as one-way traffic from the top.

The Round Table did not, happily, formulate a single recipe, suggesting that participation is a cure-all; in fact, that was not even the intention. The speakers emphasised the need for income growth, for provision of credit, for extension of basic social services, and for generating employment as well as promoting sustainable livelihoods. They showed concern for social exclusion from which many poor suffer in several countries. And, they did raise questions regarding participation from the perspective of the poor. In the true spirit of a dialogue, both the speakers and the interventionists from the audience touched upon several facets of poverty and participation but refrained from the temptation of suggesting yet another single model for the eradication of poverty.

Present mood is that of challenging available prescriptions and considering alternatives. The complacence has been shaken; the more we know about the phenomenon of poverty in different country contexts the less secure we feel in suggesting instant solutions, and the more compelled we become, as social scientists, to investigate the pervading poverty in a comparative framework.

Round Tables are not intended to offer ready-made solutions. They are the fora for generating debate and discussion. The present Round Table served that function. It agitated the minds and reminded the social science community that they have a whole lot of questions that need to be researched. There lies the challenge and the opportunity.

5

Poverty in India: A Non-Economic Perspective

Countries of the so-called Third World are passing through one of the most challenging periods of their history. The political forces unleashed in the 19th century by the emerging elite succeeded in stirring the quiescent masses to mobilise their energies against the power that held them in thrall—in their economy, their polity, their culture, and their *Weltanschauung*. The elite provided the people with the leadership that was required to expel the alien ruler and transform the country into a self-governing nation. The success of this achievement awakened, particularly among the so-called middle class, the revolution of rising expectations. Unfortunately, the inevitable gap between the level of aspirations and the level of achievements has in due course produced yet another revolution, this time one of rising frustrations. The new governments set up in these countries took upon themselves the responsibility of leading their peoples towards hope-fulfilment.

Reprinted from *Social Action,* Vol. 21, No. 1, January-March 1971, pp. 22-36. It was also published under the title "The Role of Values and Institutions" in *The Challenge of Poverty in India* (ed. A.J. Fonseca), Vikas Publications, Delhi, 1971.

They enunciated the slogan of modernising the society by making it developed and socialistic. But this goal has still to be fulfilled. India has made considerable progress on the path of economic development, but the distance that remains to be traversed is still considerable. At the present juncture, the elimination of poverty should be the main focus of Indian efforts.

In the initial phases of India's independent existence, social scientists showed as much enthusiasm as the political elite in preparing master plans for the future growth of the country. No doubt, these prescriptions and recipes of well-intentioned scholars were helpful, but they were highly unpragmatic and more in keeping with the trends of the time. In the absence of a cogently formulated theoretical model and without the basis of proper and adequate benchmark data, their prescriptions were no more than sophisticated versions of an ideological decision. Through the hard and painful process of costly failures, it is now being realised that such naive attempts are poor substitutes for a vigorous analysis of a highly complicated situation. The need for systematic studies has been severely felt and efforts in this direction are now being undertaken.

That we are still groping for a possible remedy of poverty is a good example of the failure on the part of policy makers to grasp the reality of the situation. B.N. Ganguli, in his inaugural address at a seminar, made this point very emphatically. He said:

> ...both the anatomy and physiology of poverty... (will) have to be studied in a wider frame of reference, which should be more empirical and less abstract, more micro-social and micro-economic and less macro-social and macro-economic. It is also now more clear that poverty is a typical case of plurality of causes and heterogeneous inter-mixture of effects... What... is not realized is that we tend to emphasise one cause, or a group of causes centred round a simple cause, according to our own predilections. Our minds may be influenced by ideology or

may be, as planners or as persons concerned with social action, we show such a preference subconsciously, because the corresponding remedy is socially and politically more feasible.

In the Indian context, it was a part of the new creed to imagine that a key to success is the path to *modernisation.* Encompassing a wide variety of processes, modernisation was, and is, viewed as something which is diametrically opposed to tradition. The exercise in development was, thus, designed to pursue a relentless attack on tradition and win unconditional support for modernity. Consequently, all the failures in the field of economic development were too easily attributed to tradition. During the colonial period, the foreign governments did not take steps to improve the lot of their subjects on the plea that a "tradition-bound" people could not undertake this journey. Following in their footsteps, our contemporary analysts have tried to discover the flaws in traditions which, according to them, have created innumerable bottlenecks. Therefore, while assessing the role of values and institutions in the process of modernisation, of which economic development is a part, it is necessary to discuss briefly the very concept of modernisation.

Compared to the so-called developed countries of the West, the newly liberated nations have suffered several disadvantages. A dichotomy of the rich and the poor, of the developed and the undeveloped or underdeveloped has been invented to categorise the countries of the world. The poor nations obviously treated their developed counterparts as the positive reference groups. This developed in them the desire to leave the company of the poor countries and strive to enter the club of the rich. Being latecomers, these nations are, however, in an advantageous position to learn from the lessons of the developed countries and not to repeat their mistakes. The inventions made in the developed countries, and the tools perfected by them are readily available for their immediate replication. Several years of experience can thus be compressed in a few and the pace of progress can be greatly accelerated.

The problem for India as a developing country is mainly how to utilise this experience most profitably. It can ill-afford the luxury of a rediscovery. It is not the *invention,* but the *importation* of ideas and technology that characterises the developmental activity in the new nations, which are *in a hurry* to catch up with their developed counterparts. In this kind of process of planned development, designed to bring about changes rapidly and on all fronts, the role of the decision-making elite is crucial. What is primary in this orientation is the ideology of development, based on pragmatic and empirical considerations. The elite has a double task: first to make a critical selection of the technology from the world market, and second to mobilise resources for its acquisition and finally its acceptance by the people. Regardless of ideological posture of the countries aiding India, we have welcomed the help and maintained a neutral position.

Having decided to import technology and the know-how—the hardware of the process of modernisation---the developing country has the task of tackling the software—the recipients of technology. Bottlenecks in the diffusion process need proper identification and systemic elimination. Problems of transforming the ethos of the people, of changing their attitude-configurations. and of modifying institutions have received recognition. Community Development Programmes (CDPs) for rural reconstruction and modernisation have been undertaken. The bureaucracy had to reorient itself to incorporate policy-formulation function. The elite of the society---the political leaders, the bureaucracy, the business class, the intellectuals (attached and unattached)---had an opportunity to define their role and play it.

A sizeable section of the elite regard economic development as the key to the fulfilment of the egalitarian ideal and a democratic polity. If the country prospers—its national average of production and of income show an upward trend—the poverty of the people will automatically be eliminated. A note of dissent to this complacent view is voiced by another sector. It may be argued that as the foreign interest in the country's economic development is heavily "stringed", so is the elite interest in economic development full of "strings". If the elite invest their capital, time and energy, they are likely to be the chief beneficiaries. Economic development may have the consequence of widening the gulf between the rich and the poor. It is not uncommon to hear that the rich are getting richer and poor poorer: in fact, the poor are poor enough to go further down the ladder.

It is in this context that the ideology of socialism may be examined. I tend to agree with the view that in the under-developed countries, the ideology of socialism is just another name for the ideology of development.

> What the various forms of socialism have in common, irrespective of their other ingredients, is an emphasis on development goals for which individuals must sacrifice. Government is seen as a main source *of development*... Socialism, then, has two aspects. In the context of its ideology, it defines modernity. In the application of its ideology, it defines social discipline...[1]

A slightly different interpretation of the situation is given by Lipset:

> As most new states lack the traditional means for rapid economic growth, they have been led in recent years to introduce large scale government planning and direct state intervention. Although such efforts are concerned with the socialist ideology, the desire to use the state to direct and speed up the processes of economic growth has deeper roots than

> ideological conviction. It rests upon the dual necessity to demonstrate effectiveness to the various groups within the polity and to display national competence to the outside world. To a considerable degree the leaders seek development as part of their more general effort to overcome feelings of national inferiority...[2]

It may be noted that Lipset made this remark while reviewing the earlier phase of economic development of the USA. Quoting Calender with approval, he considers that the USA at that time was "an early and leading example of the modern tendency to extend the activity of the state into industry."[3]

To sum up, a developing country gets involved in a two-fold task. The country as a whole enters into the phase of economic development to improve the country's image and to become a self-sustaining, viable political entity. Within the country, the criterion of "social justice" prompts the political machine to eradicate the poverty of individual citizens. The country's economic development lays emphasis on production; its social development lays emphasis on equitable distribution. The state's intervention in the production process and the state's responsibility in the distribution process may lead one to describe the system as characterised by a "socialistic pattern". Since the emphasis is placed on rationality and on a break with the past, the entire process may be designated as modernisation.

In clarifying the implications of modernisation we have already hinted at one form of poverty, namely, the poverty of the nation as a whole—poor resources, low GNP, weak defence and so on. The distinction between rich and poor can be made within a country as well. When we measure per capita income as a proportion of the national income distributed equally among all the citizens, we are referring to the nation's economic position. The fact of the matter is that national income is *never distributed equally*. And, this is the main source of inequality within the country. Those receiving less remain poor, and those receiving more belong to the class of the rich. Viewed in this perspective, poverty is a concept that refers to the phenomenon of relative deprivation. A highly accentuated form of deprivation is destitution that defines the economic condition of that class of people who are below the line of poverty. The destitutes do not even get that critical minimum which is essential for proper human existence. A fire-fighting approach, so vigorously advocated by those who have a concern for human values, is needed to ameliorate the conditions of these people. And, in a democratic state, with a bias in favour of a socialistic pattern of society, it is obviously the responsibility of the state to take care of these people.

Students of social stratification tell us that it is even theoretically not possible to conceive of a society without inequality. It is difficult to realise the utopian ideal of a classless society, where all ranks are eliminated and social inequality is completely erased. Inequality exists in both types of systems—class or caste. If ascription tends to *perpetuate* the phenomenon of inequality, achievement-orientation *creates* new forms of inequality. However, the dichotomy of class and caste as consisting of two incompatible types of stratification is not empirically tenable. Indian society offers an excellent example of a stratification system where the two modes of inequality have so remarkably meshed. The internal structure of caste is characterised by class level differentiations, and there are also classes which cut across the boundaries of castes.

This particular feature needs to be underlined. In devising a strategy for the abolition of poverty, if the target is fixed so high as to correspond with a perfectly egalitarian system, then it will always remain an unattainable goal. The utopian image of a classless and casteless society may be charming and attractive but is certainly a fruitless stimulus. It is, however, not the purport of this paper to suggest even latently a position of *status quo*. How must these two propositions be reconciled?

The values of egalitarianism and achievement form a syndrome of a modern society. Democracy gives expression to this value system in the field of polity, and socialism in the economic sphere. The studies relative to *elites* in society have tried to challenge the premises both of democracy and socialism. Pareto,[4] Mosca,[5] and Robert Michels[6] have come out with the argument that societies of all types have an elite class in them. The discussion of elite and non-elite in the work of Pareto, of ruling class and the rest in the writings of Mosca, and the famous *iron law* of oligarchy identified by Michels in his analysis of the German democratic system—all point towards this aspect of stratification, which is basically inegalitarian.[7] The elite group with its superior placement is the group that has all the power and perquisites. Similarly, the extension and growth of achievement orientation injects among people a spirit of competition. Since people differ in their natural endowments, they are also likely to succeed differently in the competition. And, the price of competition is the resultant inequality.

In a country with a very high level of illiteracy, the role and responsibility of running a government and leading the country on the path of economic growth and affluence is likely to rest on a small minority of elite. They possess knowledge and whatever know-how that is available. And knowledge is power. Political power may make them economically strong, or economic power may help them become politically influential.

A situation like this poses the key questions: Is the country to pursue its programme of economic development or is it to follow the principle of egalitarian distribution? Are these two either-or propositions? Can both these be pursued simultaneously in a democratic frame?

Examples are not difficult to find to illustrate the point that "economic growth is not necessarily in harmonious accord with democratic imperatives. Indeed, successful economic growth does not always promote democratic ideals; and ideals of egalitarianism may appear to hinder rather than assist economic growth."[8]

Western scholars who have regarded economic development as a precondition to the success of democracy, may lead one to infer that economic development ought to be given priority. Once economic development takes place, the forces of democracy will automatically emerge on the scene. Analysts of the Indian democratic performance may, however, hold a different view. Whatever might have been our score on the scale of economic development, we have successfully survived as a democracy. In fact, it is the democratic set-up which has greatly accelerated the pace of economic development.

Economic development of the country or region should be separated from the equitable distribution of her affluence among the people. It is precisely here that the challenge of poverty lies. Of course, this is not to deny the importance of continuing economic development of the country.

Data are available to indicate that economic growth by itself does not lead to equitable distribution. Thus, Richard Titmuss[9] has presented an impressive body of data to reveal that during the last two or three decades equalisation of income in Britain has been more apparent than real. Speaking in more general terms, John Westergaard[10] has challenged the view that there is any real basis for saying that social inequalities in Britain have been substantially reduced since the war. And there is the well-known view of C. Wright Mills[11] that in mid-twentieth century America class divisions are becoming more, and not less, rigid.[12]

Satish Arora cites several examples from the Indian scene. The Community Development Programmes have benefited more the already rich. The package programmes not merely aid villages in areas already containing basic amenities, but also help farmers who are already prosperous. The Industrial Licensing Committee noted that the largest industrial concerns have been the key beneficiaries. Arora gives French and American illustrations to complete the picture. In France, the "national income held by the lowest 30 per cent on the wage scale fell from 6.3 per cent to 4.8 per cent, while the top 10 per cent increased their share from 34.1 per cent to 36.8 per cent. Similarly, in the US, despite "the growth in national income between 1947 and 1967, total money income going to the lowest quintile of families rose only three-tenths of one per cent, that is, from 5.1 to 5.4 per cent."[13]

Pranab Bardhan, in his article on "Green Revolution and Agricultural Labourers" *(Economic & Political Weekly,* July 1970, pp. 123-26), very convincingly brings out the disparity between growth and distribution. He questions "the official view that the only feasible as well as the surest way of improving the economic condition of the weaker sections of the rural population is to encourage faster agricultural growth through subsidisation of the chemical-biological breakthrough in production and through promotion of agrarian capitalism in the countryside."

Credit must go to the famous German sociologist Max Weber for inspiring analysts to view economic development as a dependent variable. It is this style of argument which would say that capitalism succeeded in the USA because of the Protestant Ethic; similarly, failures of programmes of economic development in Asian societies have conveniently been explained by dubbing their social systems as *traditional.* It is doubtless true that programmes lacking proper appreciation of the non-economic parameters are likely to suffer frustration, but it is not quite the same thing as regarding every social structure and its culture as essentially inhibiting change. Successful engineering of change requires identification of the hard and soft points of a culture, and a skill to exploit this knowledge about the social and cultural structure in the programme for change.

In the context of Indian society, these remarks are extremely pertinent. It has been the office of the Indologist to present a book view of Indian society conceived as *exclusively* Hindu. Borrowing this convenient model, western sociologists provided India a place of honour as a rigid, socially immobile system in striking contrast with their own flexible and mobile one.

> Briefly, the older picture... described a society in which religious values and ideas were the sole determinants of attitudes toward, and chances for, social mobility in which little if any such mobility actually occurred; in which there were no discrepancies or incongruities between an individual's position in the "caste" dimension and his position in other social dimensions; in which there was practically no social change and resultant consequences for the alteration of the positions of individuals in the society; and in which in sum, a state of near-perfect integration, stability, and individual immobility prevailed for endless centuries, even millennia.[14]

The reality of Indian society compared with this picture provides a significant contrast. Thanks to the efforts of field-oriented scientists, the newly emerging picture of Indian society is in close proximity with reality. The differences in the formal outlines of Hinduism and religion as practised by the majority of Hindus are considerable; these have been attracting the attention of researchers. These differences are to be seen both in the *institutional-structural* sphere and in the *ideological-valuational* dimension.

The diversity in the social structure and social institutions obtaining in Indian society had been emphasised by many.

These diversities are the result of a wide variety of factors—regional, ethnic, religious. The communities of tribals (numbering more than 212), for instance, provide a colourful range of social structural arrangements and institutional complexes. Religious groups afford us another dimension of diversity in values and in institutions. Similarly, the concept of *spread,* advanced by M.N. Srinivas, invites us to identify the distinction between local, regional and all-India patterns.

Such "plurality, heterogeneity, or even conflict in values" are to be regarded as characteristic of the Indian system. Thus, Silverberg writes:

> A great heterogeneity of values is present and, indeed, seems to have been present in India for a long time.[15]

Similarly, Pohlman argues:

> The conflict in values and the unwillingness of low castes to accept their lowly position today, raises the question whether belief in *karma* and the like—the fatalistic acceptance of hierarchical rigidity associated with religious philosophy in India—was even really so overwhelming that all accented the system...[16]

Marriott reinforces the same point and advances a different argument:

> We must take past diversity, conflicting values, into account if we are correctly to assess the role of similar diversity in our formulations of the present caste system and in our predictions for the future... "The caste system" as a whole has been a very broad, pluralistic system made up of many queues of castes aligned behind various values. In the past, these reveal that alignments have been only partially integrated through local and regional accommodations and through intellectual speculation.

> ... (We) must note that (today) there is coming to be a much greater uniformity in the values relevant to stratification. Uniformity is a concomitant of spreading modern networks of mass communication, and an effect of having stronger governments in control of communications. A voter or a schoolboy or an ambitious group of low-caste industrial workers is no longer offered a wide variety of *varna* models for conduct. Instead, a common package of civic virtues is held up for emulation by all.[17]

I deliberately chose to quote these authorities *in extenso* to suggest the new trend in stratification analysis relative to India. As would appear from the statements quoted above, a need is felt to distinguish between verbalised values and practised values (a point on which Y.B. Damle made a specific remark in the colloquium on Social Mobility, see ibid., p.118). This means two things: *First*, those values which are noted in the scriptures are not necessarily the ones that are shared and practised by people. For one thing, they are not a part of a single system of thought; also it is too much to assume that all the people know about them---a survey of cognitive orientations of the people will be needed to describe the *spread of* these values. *Secondly,* the values inscribed in the religious texts reflect the upper caste view. For instance, vegetarianism, teetotalism, monogamy, taboo against widow remarriage, etc., are the values of the ritually upper stratum of society. The values of lower castes in regard to these aspects are very close to the western-modern ideal.

It should also be emphasised that all the traditional values need not be regarded as an antidote to modernisation. All of them are not non-rational or irrational either. Rudolphs have described this for us in their *Modernity of Tradition.*[18]

Dube has argued that traditional values contain "several elements that can be successfully utilised for promotion of economic growth". He has very cogently argued the case for such an exercise:

> Viewed historically (the) interpretations and emphases (of *dharma)* have changed. In the context of the requirements of economic development, which is a new manifestation of *artha* and *kama,* the norms of *karma* can be adopted to the new ethos. Similarly, the doctrine of *karma* does not rule out individual volition completely. In fact, it encourages it within certain limits to improve the prospects of an individual's future. The emphasis on steadfast devotion to duty irrespective of its consequences provides a base for determined and disciplined action that can be effectively utilised for realising the goals of economic development.[19]

While the dissolution of caste[20] appears to be a distant probability, several significant changes are to be noticed in the caste system. It has been pointed out by several scholars that caste and occupation are no longer synonyms. Even in the past, it is doubtful that there was such a one-to-one relationship. The politicisation of caste has been a recent phenomenon. Formation of caste associations and exploitation of the caste sentiment for political gains have significantly affected the worldview of the people; they have developed skills in empathy, and they are increasingly becoming confident of their being politically efficacious. Education, industrialisation and urban impact have made mobility possible and the number of parvenus is getting larger and larger. Discontentment arising out of the present position has become a characteristic feature of the present-day individual. If discontentment is regarded as a precondition to personal advancement, then the forces tending to generate it must be strengthened and institutionalised.

It may be argued that a democratic set-up provides such an apparatus. The mechanisms to articulate the aggregative interests of the people are made available in a democracy. Political parties, interest groups and pressure groups may be regarded as the needed organisational structures; faith in democracy, regard for a better standard of living, and achievement orientation are the attendant values to be promoted. Systematic investigations are needed in different parts of the country, and among different strata, to provide information on these points. In what measure have these values been *internalised,* and by whom? Who are the people who are yet docile and contented? What are the directions of mobility?

It should be categorically stated that in the analysis of poverty, heavy reliance on caste as an *independent* variable is likely to be misleading. To the extent that it has provided a ritual dimension of hierarchy, caste becomes only secondarily relevant to the question of economic inequality. Economic inequalities are to be noticed in families as units; ritual inequality treats castes as units. Individual members of a caste can move up or down the wealth ladder and thereby create class distinctions within the caste. Ignoring this fact, the government formulated the policy of giving special privileges to the scheduled castes and backward classes. Given with the intention of improving the lot of these people and bringing them at par with other groups these privileges, granted by the government wedded to the ideal of a casteless and classless society, have served the two-fold function of fostering the solidarity of the caste and at the same time widening the gulf between the rich and the poor within the same caste. The other consequence has been the neglect of those "poor" persons who unfortunately were not born in these low castes.

The reference made to the government in the previous paragraph should help in appreciating the point that the role of institutions and values needs to be examined at three levels:

1. Economic development of the country: Plan and priorities

How are the goals of economic development to be defined? What is the relative significance of a particular form of polity and the type of economic development? Which are the reference models?

How to reinterpret the values of other societies treated as reference models, and how to transform their institutions? These questions are the bother of the elite. The conflicting values of the ruling and the non-ruling elite at the apex will have to be studied to describe the process of goal-definition.

2. Economic development: Implementation of the plan

The implementation of the plans involves the bureaucracy on the one hand and the people on the other. One may also include the intermediate category of intellectual elite. The values of the bureaucrat and the institutional apparatus of his office may help or hinder developmental activity. Likewise, the involvement of the people in developmental activity depends on their *acceptance* of the goals of the programme, and their perception of these goals as overlapping with their personal goals.

3. Individual's orientation to social mobility

Apart from the paternalistic attitude shown by the elite to the poor person, the latter may or may not be motivated to move up. Conversely, despite his keen desire to move up, if the opportunity structure of the society does not promote his ambition and provide channels for mobility, he is likely to feel frustrated and to be forced to remain where he is.

Analyses of India's economic development bring home the point that there are several flaws in the first two levels. The gaps between the intention and the strategy employed to accomplish them have been pointed out by many scholars. Similarly, gaps are to be found in the values of the bureaucrat or the technical man and the goals of the society. It is a very hard and painful exercise for the bureaucrat to redefine himself as the *servant* of the people. Similarly, the doctor, the agricultural graduate or the engineer is more concerned about his urban comforts and least bothered about his role as a specialist in the rural sector. The people still view the government as solely responsible *for* carrying out programmes for development. The ambivalence in regard to government---both as *mai-baap* and as people's servant---is widely prevalent.

Despite all this, individual ambition is rising higher. The gap that separates the rich from the poor is not only noticed but is also regarded as something undesirable.

The Government of India took several measures to improve the economic life of the people living in rural areas. These measures relate to the improvement of agriculture, reform of land relations, provision of credit facilities, well-rounded development of the community through CDP and NES and promotion of cottage and small-scale industries. The consequences of all these measures have been mixed. To quote A.R. Desai:

> ... great changes have taken place in the socio-economic structure of the rural society. Some of the old classes (feudal and semi-feudal) have been largely crippled; some (substantial) farmers have been strengthened. Middle and lower sections have not benefited. The process of economic disintegration of these sections is advancing. (i) The measures have resulted in transforming many *zamindar* type of landlords into a class of substantial farmers and capitalist agriculturists. (ii) By numerous tenancy and other laws... the government is helping to create a class of prosperous peasants out of substantial tenants or a section of the medium-sized cultivators.
>
> On the other hand, the vast mass of unemployed persons, large sections of the owners of uneconomic holdings, the mass of poor peasants and agricultural labourers either remain unaffected by these measures or are adversely affected.[21]

It may be the precipitation of these processes that activities like the Naxalite movement and the land-grab movement have caught the fancy of the people. Their predecessor, non-violent *Bhoodan,* was also an effort in the same direction. A careful analysis of these trends is necessary to appreciate their impact and to work out a suitable strategy to curb them and to provide alternative means to fulfil the ambition of the people for which these movements were launched.

The common man has entered the "orbit of desire", and is increasingly becoming "secular" in his approach. Institutions and values that govern his social relations in the traditional sphere have acquired a new mix. To some, he is attached; against others, he is revolting. The institutional complex and the implementation mechanism at the governmental level have not been able to cope with the situation. The situation is infinitely complex; it cannot be understood and improved by taking a worn-out textbook view and finding faults with the social structure and culture.

The above analysis hints at the necessity of an objective cartography of the value profile of the people of the different strata of society. It also remains to be discovered whether all the persons having the same value profile belong to the same socio-economic status category. It should not be forgotten that adherents to Hindu values are not all poor; and if people belonging to the lower (and poor) class have values that are different from the official values of the Hindu religion, then an explanation will have to be established for their poverty. As a hypothesis, it appears that the values cherished by the "already-rich" have served as "inhibitions" (in the sense in which Myrdal uses the term) to launch any programme of equalisation or upliftment. The poor, who may have accepted the ideology of the dominant group at one point of time, are clearly swinging on the ocean of aspirations. What is the extent to which a poor man can attain some of his goals will depend upon the availability of legitimate means.

The opening of the avenues of mobility will thus give an opportunity to the person to rise or fall. The rise will make him rich, the fall will bring him to the culture of poverty. Let us recognise, then, that in this kind of system, too, every one will not be born with a silver spoon in his mouth. Competition and achievement will initiate a cycle of status change but not eliminate inequality. The principle of equal or equitable distribution, without regard to the recipient's merit, will be an indirect reinforcement of the ascription principle.

The burden of my argument then is the following: it is possible to ameliorate the condition of a particular person, but it is not possible to abolish the phenomenon of poverty. If the premise is granted, effort should be made to provide those conditions which facilitate a person to become "rich". A proper frame of mind, congenial milieu, and access to legitimate means for ascendancy are the requisites. In the process of economic development of the country, the state's direct intervention is the prime necessity. Implicit in the analysis is also the suggestion that the nation's economic development is no guarantee of the abolition of ranks and strata within the society.

Notes

1. David Apter, *Ideology and Discontent,* The Free Press of Glencoe, 1964, p.23
2. S.M. Lipset, *The First New Nation,* New York: Basic Books Inc., 1963, p. 46.
3. Ibid., p. 48.

4. Vilfredo Pareto, *The Mind and Society* (4 vols.), Jonathan Cape, 1935.
5. Gaetano Mosca, *The Ruling Class,* New York: McGraw Hill, 1939.
6. Robert Michels, *Political Parties,* Glencoe, The Free Press, 1949.
7. See T.B. Bottomore, *Elites and Society,* New York: Basic Books, 1964.
8. Satish K. Arora, "Economic Growth, Social Justice and Political Stability", *Economic and Political Weekly,* Special Number, July 1970, p. 1203.
9. R.M. Titmuss, *Income Distribution and Social Change,* Allen & Unwin, 1962.
10. J.H. Westergaard, "The Withering Away of Class, a Contemporary Myth", in Perry Anderson et al. *Towards Socialism,* London, 1965.
11. C. Wright Mills, *White Collar,* Oxford University Press, 1953; *The Power Elite,* Oxford University Press, 1959.
12. A. Beteille, *Social Inequality,* Penguin, 1969, p. 363.
13. Satish K. Arora, op. cit. For France, Arora refers to Gilbert Mathieu, "France where the Rich are Richer", *Le Monde,* June 10, 1970. For US, see Pamela Roby, "Inequality: A Trend Analysis", *The Annals of the American Academy of Political and Social Sciences,* Vol. 385, September 1969, p. 113.
14. Bernard Barber, "Social Mobility in Hindu India", in *Social Mobility in the Caste System in India,* ed. J. Silverberg, Comparative Studies in Society and History, Supplement, III, Mouton: The Hague, p. 18.
15. James Silverberg, *Social Mobility in the Caste System in India,* op. cit., p. 117.
16. Ibid.
17. Ibid., p. 119.
18. Lloyd I. Rudolph and Susanne H. Rudolph, *The Modernity of Tradition: Political Development in India,* The University of Chicago Press, 1967.

19. S.C. Dube, "Cultural Problems in Economic Development as Observed in Land Reform, Community Development, the Industrialization Process and the Family Concept in Hindu Society". Paper presented in an International Seminar on *Cultural Motivations to Progress,* University of Philippines, Manila, 1963, p. 5.
20. See Yogesh Atal, *The Changing Frontiers of Caste,* Delhi: National Publishing House, 1968.
21. A.R. Desai, "Impact of Governmental Measures on Rural Society", in *Rural Sociology in India* (ed. Desai), Bombay: Popular Book Depot, 1969, p. 775.

    See also in the same volume, Sulekh Chandra Gupta, "Some Aspects of Indian Agriculture", pp. 291-327.

6

Weaker Sections: The Sociological Dimension

Immediately upon independence, in our quest for a new and a different India, we launched several activities under the rubric "development". While we planned, our approach remained sectoral---for each activity we developed a long-range agenda, and in most of them it is the "economic" which dominated. The integrative character of the social system and the non-rational element in social behaviour did not receive adequate attention under the spell of economic supremacy. This has also been the case with our approach towards the so-called "weaker sections".

A common error in our approach to development has been to equate inequalities in the economic sphere with social inequalities. Having identified the lowly groups in the caste hierarchy of the Hindus, we have listed them in a schedule and granted them special privileges in the political and economic spheres with the express hope that this would ameliorate their ritually degraded status.

Paper presented in a Seminar on *Rural Development for Weaker Sections*, held at Indian Institute of Management, Ahmedabad in October 1972.

Associated with this style of reasoning is the use of a rather simplistic kind of dichotomy through which all the castes in village India are classified into either the landed or the landless ---a version of the *haves* and *have-nots* dichotomy.

Prescriptions to cure the "social maladies" suggested by scholars accepting the above-mentioned premises have no doubt been unrealistic and non-pragmatic.

It is wrong to equate poverty with ascriptive status: there are poor families among the castes which are traditionally assigned a high status; similarly, there are top-achievers among the so-called scheduled castes and scheduled tribes.

We should also be clear that weaker sections (as the term is understood) are not the exclusive preserve of the Hindu—among the Muslims and Christians, too, one can trace the spread of poverty.

Being landless need not always be interpreted as being poor. Even the tradition of caste society identifies a wide variety of occupations that are somehow bound with individual castes. In this framework, agriculture figures, by and large, as a caste-free occupation. Occupations other than agriculture and traditionally associated with castes may be (or may not be) directly or indirectly dependent upon agriculture. Participation in agriculture by clean or unclean artisan and service rendering castes has largely been in the nature of a secondary occupation. Analyses that tended to ignore this fact have luxuriously indulged in vulgar characterisation of unemployment.

Take, for instance, the concept of agricultural labour. People falling in this category are generally described as "landless". But this concept has been used as a catch-all expression. The definition has varied from census to census, and from one enquiry to another. Thus, in the 1951 census of India, it was meant for all "employees of cultivators" irrespective of whether they were engaged in crop production, or in horticulture, dairy farming, herding cattle, house construction, sinking wells, or even when they were "non-earning" dependants. In the census of 1961, the non-earning dependants were excluded, and persons working on another's land on wages (cash or kind) were classed as agricultural labour. In the Agricultural Labour Enquiry, conducted in 1950-51, the agricultural labourer was defined as a person who was employed for wages in crop production and who spent more than half of his total days of work in a year on this job. In another similar enquiry, conducted in 1956-57, people engaged on hire or exchange in any of the following occupations were classed as agricultural labourers: farming, dairy, horticulture, raising of livestock (including bees and poultry). In addition, all those persons who were owners of land but whose income from their land was less than 50 per cent of the total income, and who were supplementing it by working on others' fields were also included.

Owing to the differences in definition, the actual estimates of agricultural labour have varied. This may be the reason, or at least one of the reasons, for the anomalous datum supplied by the 1971 census in regard to Bihar where the size of agricultural labourers has grown out of all proportions during the decade 1961-1971.

Definitional crisis also haunts the other sector classified as the "weaker section", namely, scheduled castes and scheduled tribes. It has not been possible so far to consolidate a uniform set of criteria for purposes of scheduling. Untouchability, lower ritual status, unclean occupations, poverty, lack of education, general backwardness, nomadism and similar factors have generally gone into the decision-making for inclusion of a given caste into the schedule. Thus, by evolving a schedule for all such castes who suffer from one or more of the disabilities listed above, we have succeeded in a "lump-together" exercise. The word "Harijan"[*] designates this cluster of castes.

* Somewhere in the 1980s this word got dropped and replaced by another, namely, "Dalit".

Let it be understood that the decision to evolve a schedule and to put castes of certain rank in it is a political one. While not involved in the rationale for such a schedule, the academia have responded to the invitation and several of the scholars have attempted analyses by treating the "lump" as a "given" social group. The pitfalls in such an analysis are too obvious. We may briefly dwell upon this issue.

Untouchability admits of degrees. All the castes included in the schedule do not suffer from the same degree of untouchability. Instances have been cited where some untouchable groups have not figured in the schedule; and others who are not untouchable have found a place. Sheer fact of conversion has been regarded, in some cases, as abolition of untouchability. Sections of castes, or individuals who converted to Christianity, or to Islam, or to Sikhism, could not shed their caste identity and they continue to suffer from indignities.

Unclean occupations, likewise, have a hierarchy. While these occupations may be caste-bound in the sense that they can be undertaken only by persons of a given caste, not all the persons belonging to that caste engage themselves in that occupation.

Attribution of poverty at the group level assumes equal distribution of resources and income among all the members of the group. Since scheduled castes are not one group but are a cluster of many groups, the extent of poverty in each of the groups will have to be separately determined; however, the "average" arrived at for a given scheduled caste will be a meaningless datum owing to the unequal distribution. Poverty is to be located at the level of family. Understood this way, families struck by poverty or even destitution may have a much wider scatter---among all castes, different religions and regions, and in rural and urban areas.

Programmes of rural development in India mainly concentrated on two aspects, namely, agriculture and weaker sections. In the initial period of India's journey towards development, the emphasis was on the growth of economy. Quite understandably, the index of this growth was GNP. Division of GNP by the size of the country's population has provided an idea of per capita income which has shown a steady rise over the years. Comparison of this figure with the countries of the developed world makes one feel distressed; the entire nation is poor compared to the many affluent countries of the West. Removal of the poverty of the nation requires economic growth with GNP as a measure, but a rich nation does not ensure absence of poor families.

Lack of harmonious accord between economic growth and socialistic ideal of distributive justice has been suggested by numerous observers of the western scene. Over the years, with the growth of economy, income disparities and economic inequalities in countries like UK, USA and France have increased. Community Development Programmes (CDPs) in India have contributed to the prosperity of the already advantaged---be they villages or families. Faster agricultural growth under the spell of the Green Revolution also seems to have promoted agrarian capitalism.

It is on the foundations of these hard facts that Gunnar Myrdal has taken a different view in his outline of a world antipoverty programme presented in *The Challenge of World Poverty,* published in 1970. Myrdal does not regard the twin goals of economic growth and economic equality as conflicting. He cogently argues "why greater equality in underdeveloped countries is almost a condition for more rapid growth" (p. 68). His argument may be summarised as under:

1. "the usual argument that inequality of income is a condition for saving has much less bearing on conditions in underdeveloped countries, where landlords and other rich people are known to squander their incomes for conspicuous consumption and conspicuous investment..."

2. "since large masses of people in underdeveloped countries suffer from undernutrition, malnutrition, and other serious defects, in their level of living... measures to raise income levels for the masses of people would raise productivity..."
3. "social inequality is tied to economic inequality in a mutual relationship..."
4. "behind the quest for greater equality is the recognition of the fact that it has an independent value in terms of social justice..."

It appears upon evaluation that in India the two goals were pursued independently with a relatively greater stress on economic growth. With the new slogan of *Garibi Hatao,* the Indian government seems to be in a mood to shift its emphasis from economic growth to social justice and economic equality. Such a shift is recognition of the fact that our planning paid only a lip service to the equality goal. It also suggests that prescription of simultaneous pursuit of the two goals is not yet acceptable. If it had been unfortunate to give secondary status to distributive justice in the past, it will equally be disastrous to declare a holiday for economic growth. There must be a quest for a judicious mix of the two.

In attempting such a mix that will inform our development certain points will have to be kept in view:

1. It will be necessary to define the concept of economic equality. The sense that averaging of GNP conveys is not to be confused with the concrete realities of life. It is just not possible to create a society with no strata, no classes, no income disparities. Poverty defined in terms of *relative deprivation* will continue to exist; we may reduce the strata, and the gaps between them, but we cannot eliminate them.
2. Destitution should be distinguished from poverty and the measures to eliminate it should be evaluated not in terms of

their immediate economic cost but in terms of their long-range social cost.

3. Poverty and destitution should be dealt with either in terms of a geographical region, or at the level of the family. The caste approach followed so far is clearly wrong. Both education and income show their influence on the individual and his family. Incomes are not combined to enhance the status of caste, nor does literacy percentage computed at the caste level change the social position of the caste. There is, thus, a need to question the thesis that economic betterment and educational advancement would result in closure of caste cleavages on the ritual frontier.
4. If caste is considered an obstacle, and therefore undesirable, recognition of it as a unit for disbursement of governmental privileges is certainly ill-advised. It has resulted into strengthening of caste at the lower level and emergence of a renovated casteism.
5. Laying emphasis on status rise in caste hierarchy, or on temple entry is contrary to secular ideal. Efforts made to force entry of Harijans into the temple were, in fact, misguided. It only meant an indirect support of the governmental agency to the ethos of caste and the worldview of the Hindu.
6. Following caste approach and reserving seats in educational institutions and in governmental positions, as well as in legislative chambers is a vestige of the British policy, namely, representation to minorities. The consequences of that policy have been amply dysfunctional. In the same fashion, special privileges granted to them have developed in them an unfortunate vested interest in remaining backward. Rather than feeling pride in getting out of the schedule they jealously guard that position, and envied by their privileged position many other castes have made attempts to enter into

the list. Today, it is difficult to deschedule any caste; tomorrow it will be almost impossible, and the schedule may go on becoming larger and larger.

7. The caste approach cannot be replaced by class. While caste has a group character, class is an ideal construct of the theorist. In reality, it is the families which can be categorised in terms of their economic position; and the deserving cases irrespective of their caste status should get fuller social justice. They cannot be allowed to be deprived till such time that the positions are reversed. To do so will be to invite trouble and generate tension.

If we wish to replace the limited concepts of agricultural labour and scheduled castes (one exclusively economic and the other characteristically social) by "weaker section", its definition will have to be rigorous. Mere name change will not do. In adopting a label, the ideological undertones should also be carefully analysed. Using the word "weaker", we are, on the one hand, suggesting a dichotomy in which the other pole is inhabited by the "strong", and, on the other, injecting a sense of inferiority among the so-called "weaker". The cumulativeness implied in a composite concept like this may itself be questionable. Does weakness in any one of the indicators imply weakness in the rest? Do we assume a very high coefficient of reproducibility? Moreover, in between the strong and the weak, there may be several groups of "not-so-strong" or "not-so-weak" type. Imputing a group attribute is to ignore a scatter. The patronising attitude of the elite expressed in terms of concessions granted to the "so far deprived" people goes contrary to the democratic principle and goes a long way in fostering an oligarchy.

Most of our developmental activities are directed at the level of the family; even the privileges granted to special groups are distributed at the family level: land reforms affect landed families, literacy programmes influence individuals and their families, family planning programmes also focus at the family. Aggregating all the advantages or disadvantages at the caste level may make the statistics impressive and the economics dismal, but its sociology is indeed vulgar.

I would opt for an area approach using a systems framework. It is time that caste is delinked from economic planning. The twin goals of economic growth and economic equality need to be pursued in any programmes that are prepared for specific regions taking the total context into account.

Slogans may provide stimulus to a scholar but they should not spell his strategy.

Appendix

The Copenhagen Declaration and Programme of Action

Chapter 2: Eradication of Poverty

World Summit for Social Development, 6-12 March 1995

ERADICATION OF POVERTY

Basis for action and objectives

18. Over 1 billion people in the world today live under unacceptable conditions of poverty, mostly in developing countries, and particularly in rural areas of low-income Asia and the Pacific, Africa, Latin America and the Caribbean, and the least developed countries.

19. Poverty has various manifestations, including lack of income and productive resources sufficient to ensure sustainable livelihoods; hunger and malnutrition; ill health; limited or lack of access to education and other basic services; increased morbidity and mortality from illness; homelessness and inadequate housing; unsafe environments; and social discrimination and exclusion. It is also characterized by a lack of participation in decision-making and in civil, social and cultural life. It occurs in all countries: as mass poverty in many developing countries, pockets of poverty amid wealth in developed countries, loss of livelihoods as a result of economic recession, sudden poverty as a result of disaster or conflict, the poverty of low-wage workers, and the utter destitution of people who fall outside family support systems, social institutions and safety nets. Women bear a disproportionate burden of poverty, and children growing up in poverty are often permanently disadvantaged. Older people, people with disabilities, indigenous people, refugees and internally displaced persons are also particularly vulnerable to poverty. Furthermore, poverty in its various forms represents a barrier to communication and access to services, as well as a major health risk, and people living in poverty are particularly vulnerable to the consequences of disasters and conflicts. Absolute poverty is a condition characterized by severe deprivation of basic human needs, including food, safe drinking water, sanitation facilities, health, shelter, education and information. It depends not only on income but also on access to social services.

20. There is general agreement that persistent widespread poverty, as well as serious social and gender inequities, have significant influences on and are in turn

influenced by demographic parameters, such as population growth, structure and distribution. There is also general agreement that unsustainable consumption and production patterns are contributing to the unsustainable use of natural resources and environmental degradation, as well as to the reinforcement of social inequities and poverty, with the above-mentioned consequences for demographic parameters.

21. Urban poverty is rapidly increasing in pace with overall urbanization. It is a growing phenomenon in all countries and regions, and often poses special problems, such as overcrowding, contaminated water and bad sanitation, unsafe shelter, crime and additional social problems. An increasing number of low-income urban households are female-maintained.

22. Among people living in poverty, gender disparities are marked, especially in the increase in female-maintained households. With increasing population, the numbers of youth living in poverty will increase significantly. Therefore, specific measures are needed to address the juvenilization and feminization of poverty.

23. Poverty has various causes, including structural ones. Poverty is a complex multidimensional problem with origins in both the national and international domains. No uniform solution can be found for global application. Rather, country-specific programmes to tackle poverty and international efforts supporting national efforts, as well as the parallel process of creating a supportive international environment, are crucial for a solution to this problem. Poverty is inseparably linked to lack of control over resources, including land, skills, knowledge, capital and social connections. Without those resources, people are easily neglected by policy makers and have limited access to institutions, markets, employment and public services. The eradication of poverty cannot be accomplished through

anti-poverty programmes alone but will require democratic participation and changes in economic structures in order to ensure access for all to resources, opportunities and public services, to undertake policies geared to more equitable distribution of wealth and income, to provide social protection for those who cannot support themselves, and to assist people confronted by unforeseen catastrophe, whether individual or collective, natural, social or technological.

24. The eradication of poverty requires universal access to economic opportunities that will promote sustainable livelihood and basic social services, as well as special efforts to facilitate access to opportunities and services for the disadvantaged. People living in poverty and vulnerable groups must be empowered through organization and participation in all aspects of political, economic and social life, in particular in the planning and implementation of policies that affect them, thus enabling them to become genuine partners in development.

25. There is therefore an urgent need for:

- National strategies to reduce overall poverty substantially, including measures to remove the structural barriers that prevent people from escaping poverty, with specific time-bound commitments to eradicate absolute poverty by a target date to be specified by each country in its national context;
- Stronger international cooperation and the support of international institutions to assist countries in their efforts to eradicate poverty and to provide basic social protection and services;
- Development of methods to measure all forms of poverty, especially absolute poverty, and to assess and monitor the circumstances of those at risk, within the national context;

- Regular national reviews of economic policies and national budgets to orient them towards eradicating poverty and reducing inequalities;
- Expanded opportunities to enable people living in poverty to enhance their overall capacities and improve their economic and social conditions, while managing resources sustainably;
- Human resource development and improved infrastructural facilities;
- Comprehensive provision for the basic needs of all;
- Policies ensuring that all people have adequate economic and social protection during unemployment, ill health, maternity, disability and old age;
- Policies that strengthen the family and contribute to its stability in accordance with the principles, goals and commitments contained in the Copenhagen Declaration on Social Development and in the Programme of Action of the International Conference on Population and Development;
- Mobilization of both the public and the private sectors, more developed areas, educational and academic institutions and non-governmental organizations to assist poverty-stricken areas.

Actions

A. Formulation of integrated strategies

26. Governments should give greater focus to public efforts to eradicate absolute poverty and to reduce overall poverty substantially by:

a. Promoting sustained economic growth, in the context of sustainable development, and social progress, requiring that growth be broadly based, offering equal opportunities to all people. All countries should recognize their common but differentiated responsibilities. The developed countries acknowledge the responsibility they bear in the international pursuit of sustainable development, and should continue to improve their efforts to promote sustained economic growth and to narrow imbalances in a manner that can benefit all countries, particularly the developing countries;

b. Formulating or strengthening, preferably by 1996, and implementing national poverty eradication plans to address the structural causes of poverty, encompassing action on the local, national, subregional, regional and international levels. These plans should establish, within each national context, strategies and affordable time-bound goals and targets for the substantial reduction of overall poverty and the eradication of absolute poverty. In the context of national plans, particular attention should be given to employment creation as a means of eradicating poverty, giving appropriate consideration to health and education, assigning a higher priority to basic social services, generating household income, and promoting access to productive assets and economic opportunities;

c. Identifying the livelihood systems, survival strategies and self-help organizations of people living in poverty and working with such organizations to develop programmes for combating poverty that build on their efforts, ensuring the full participation of the people concerned and responding to their actual needs;

d. Elaborating, at the national level, the measurements, criteria and indicators for determining the extent and distribution of absolute poverty. Each country should develop a precise definition and assessment of absolute poverty, preferably by 1996, the International Year for the Eradication of Poverty;

e. Establishing policies, objectives and measurable targets to enhance and broaden women's economic opportunities and their access to productive resources, particularly women who have no source of income;

f. Promoting effective enjoyment by all people of civil, cultural, economic, political and social rights, and access to existing social protection and public services, in particular through encouraging the ratification and ensuring the full implementation of relevant human rights instruments, such as the International Covenant on Economic, Social and Cultural Rights and the International Covenant on Civil and Political Rights;

g. Eliminating the injustice and obstacles that women are faced with, and encouraging and strengthening the participation of women in taking decisions and in implementing them, as well as their access to productive resources and land ownership and their right to inherit goods;

h. Encouraging and supporting local community development projects that foster the skill, self-reliance and self-confidence of people living in poverty and that facilitate their active participation in efforts to eradicate poverty.

27. Governments are urged to integrate goals and targets for combating poverty into overall economic and social policies and planning at the local, national and, where appropriate, regional levels by:

a. Analysing policies and programmes, including those relating to macroeconomic stability, structural adjustment programmes, taxation, investments, employment, markets and all relevant sectors of the economy, with respect to their impact on poverty and inequality, assessing their impact on family well-being and conditions, as well as their gender implications, and adjusting them, as appropriate, to promote a more equitable distribution of productive assets, wealth, opportunities, income and services;

b. Redesigning public investment policies that relate to infrastructure development, the management of natural resources and human resource development to benefit people living in poverty and to promote their compatibility with the long-term improvement of livelihoods;

c. Ensuring that development policies benefit low-income communities and rural and agricultural development;

d. Selecting, wherever possible, development schemes that do not displace local populations, and designing an appropriate policy and legal framework to compensate the displaced for their losses, to help them to re-establish their livelihoods and to promote their recovery from social and cultural disruption;

e. Designing and implementing environmental protection and resource management measures that take into account the needs of people living in poverty and vulnerable groups in accordance with Agenda 21 and the various consensus agreements, conventions and programmes of action adopted in the framework of the follow-up to the United Nations Conference on Environment and Development;

f. Establishing and strengthening, as appropriate, mechanisms for the coordination of efforts to combat poverty, in collaboration with civil society, including the private sector, and developing integrated intersectoral and intra-governmental responses for such purposes.

28. People living in poverty and their organizations should be empowered by:

a. Involving them fully in the setting of targets and in the design, implementation, monitoring and assessment of national strategies and programmes for poverty eradication and community-based development, and ensuring that such programmes reflect their priorities;

b. Integrating gender concerns in the planning and implementation of policies and programmes for the empowerment of women;

c. Ensuring that policies and programmes affecting people living in poverty respect their dignity and culture and make full use of their knowledge, skills and resourcefulness;

d. Strengthening education at all levels and ensuring the access to education of people living in poverty, in particular their access to primary education and other basic education opportunities;

e. Encouraging and assisting people living in poverty to organize so that their representatives can participate in economic and social policy-making and work more effectively with governmental, non-governmental and other relevant institutions to obtain the services and opportunities they need;

f. Placing special emphasis on capacity-building and community-based management;

g. Educating people about their rights, the political system and the availability of programmes.

29. There is a need to periodically monitor, assess and share information on the performance of poverty eradication plans, evaluate policies to combat poverty, and promote an understanding and awareness of poverty and its causes and consequences. This could be done, by Governments, *inter alia,* through:

a. Developing, updating and disseminating specific and agreed gender-disaggregated indicators of poverty and vulnerability, including income, wealth, nutrition, physical and mental health, education, literacy, family conditions, unemployment, social exclusion and isolation, homelessness, landlessness and other factors, as well as indicators of the national and international causes underlying poverty; for this purpose, gathering comprehensive and comparable data, disaggregated by ethnicity, gender, disability, family status, language groupings, regions and economic and social sectors;

b. Monitoring and assessing the achievement of goals and targets agreed to in international forums in the area of social development; evaluating, quantitatively and qualitatively, changes in poverty levels, the persistence of poverty, and vulnerability to poverty, particularly concerning household income levels and access to resources and services; and assessing the effectiveness of poverty eradication strategies, based on the priorities and perceptions of households living in poverty and low-income communities;

c. Strengthening international data collection and statistical systems to support countries in monitoring social development goals, and encouraging the expansion of international databases to incorporate socially beneficial activities that are not included in available data, such as women's unremunerated work and contributions to society, the informal economy and sustainable livelihoods;

d. Mobilizing public awareness, in particular through educational institutions, non-governmental organizations and the media, to enable society to prioritize the struggle against poverty, while focusing attention on progress or failure in the pursuit of defined goals and targets;

e. Mobilizing the resources of universities and research institutions to improve the understanding of the causes of poverty and their solutions, as well as the impact of structural adjustment measures on people living in poverty and the effectiveness of anti-poverty strategies and programmes, strengthening the capacity for social science research in developing countries and integrating, as appropriate, the results of research into decision-making processes;

f. Facilitating and promoting the exchange of knowledge and experience, especially among developing countries, through, *inter alia,* subregional and regional organizations.

30. Members of the international community should, bilaterally or through multilateral organizations, foster an enabling environment for poverty eradication by:

a. Coordinating policies and programmes to support the measures being taken in the developing countries, particularly in Africa and the least developed countries, to eradicate poverty, provide remunerative work and strengthen social integration in order to meet basic social development goals and targets;

b. Promoting international cooperation to assist developing countries, at their request, in their efforts, in particular at the community level, towards achieving gender equality and the empowerment of women;

c. Strengthening the capacities of developing countries to monitor the progress of national poverty eradication plans and to assess the impact of national and international policies and programmes on people living in poverty and address their negative impacts;

d. Strengthening the capacity of countries with economies in transition to develop their social protection systems and social policies for, *inter alia,* the reduction of poverty;

e. Addressing the special needs of small island developing States with respect to eradicating poverty and meeting poverty eradication goals and targets, within the context of social development programmes that reflect their national priorities;

f. Addressing the problems faced by the land-locked developing countries in eradicating poverty and supporting their efforts aimed at social development;

g. Supporting societies disrupted by conflict in their efforts to rebuild their social protection systems and eradicate poverty.

B. Improved access to productive resources and infrastructure

31. The opportunities for income generation, diversification of activities and increase of productivity in low-income and poor communities should be enhanced by:

a. Improving the availability and accessibility of transportation, communication, power and energy services at the local or community level, in particular for isolated, remote and marginalized communities;

b. Ensuring that investments in infrastructure support sustainable development at the local or community levels;

c. Emphasizing the need for developing countries that are heavily dependent on primary commodities to continue to promote a domestic policy and an institutional environment that encourage diversification and enhance competitiveness;

d. Supporting the importance of commodity diversification as a means to increase the export revenues of developing countries and to improve their competitiveness in the face of the persistent instability in the price of some primary commodities and the general deterioration in the terms of trade;

e. Promoting, including by micro-enterprises, rural non-farm production and service activities, such as agro-processing, sales and services of agricultural equipment and inputs, irrigation, credit services and other income-generating activities through, *inter alia,* supportive laws and administrative measures, credit policies, and technical and administrative training;

f. Strengthening and improving financial and technical assistance for community-based development and self-help programmes, and, strengthening cooperation among Governments, community organizations, cooperatives, formal and informal banking institutions, private enterprises and international agencies, with the aim of mobilizing local savings, promoting the creation of local financial networks, and increasing the availability of credit and market information to small entrepreneurs, small farmers and other low-income self-employed workers, with particular efforts to ensure the availability of such services to women;

g. Strengthening organizations of small farmers, landless tenants and labourers, other small producers, fisherfolk, community-based and workers' cooperatives, especially those run by women, in order to, *inter alia,* improve market access and increase productivity, provide inputs and technical advice, promote cooperation in production and marketing operations, and strengthen participation in the planning and implementation of rural development;

h. Promoting national and international assistance in providing economically viable alternatives for social groups, especially farmers involved in the cultivation and processing of crops used for the illegal drug trade;

i. Improving the competitiveness of natural products with environmental advantages and strengthening the impact that this could have on promoting sustainable consumption and production patterns, and strengthening and improving financial and technical assistance to the developing countries for research and development of such products;

j. Promoting comprehensive rural development, including by land reform, land improvement and economic diversification;

k. Improving economic opportunities for rural women through the elimination of legal, social, cultural and practical obstacles to women's participation in economic activities and ensuring that women have equal access to productive resources.

32. Rural poverty should be addressed by:

a. Expanding and improving land ownership through such measures as land reform and improving the security of land tenure, and ensuring the equal rights of women and men in this respect, developing new agricultural land, promoting fair land rents, making land transfers more efficient and fair, and adjudicating land disputes;

b. Promoting fair wages and improving the conditions of agricultural labour, and increasing the access of small farmers to water, credit, extension services and appropriate technology, including for women, persons with disabilities and vulnerable groups on the basis of equality;

c. Strengthening measures and actions designed to improve the social, economic and living conditions in rural areas and thereby discouraging rural exodus;

d. Promoting opportunities for small farmers and other agricultural, forestry and fishery workers on terms that respect sustainable development;

e. Improving access to markets and market information in order to enable small producers to obtain better prices for their products and pay better prices for the materials they need;

f. Protecting, within the national context, the traditional rights to land and other resources of pastoralists, fishery workers and nomadic and indigenous people, and strengthening land management in the areas of pastoral or nomadic activity, building on traditional communal practices, controlling encroachment by others, and developing improved systems of range management and access to water, markets, credit, animal production, veterinary services, health including health services, education and information;

g. Promoting education, research and development on farming systems and smallholder cultivation and animal husbandry techniques, particularly in environmentally fragile areas, building on local and traditional practices of sustainable agriculture and taking particular advantage of women's knowledge;

h. Strengthening agricultural training and extension services to promote a more effective use of existing technologies and indigenous knowledge systems and to disseminate new technologies in order to reach both men and women farmers and other agricultural workers, including through the hiring of more women as extension workers;

i. Promoting infrastructural and institutional investment in small-scale farming in resource-poor regions so that small-scale farmers can fully explore market opportunities, within the context of liberalization.

33. Access to credit by small rural or urban producers, landless farmers and other people with low or no income should be substantially improved, with special attention to the needs of women and disadvantaged and vulnerable groups, by:

a. Reviewing national legal, regulatory and institutional frameworks that restrict the access of people living in poverty, especially women, to credit on reasonable terms;

b. Promoting realistic targets for access to affordable credit, where appropriate;

c. Providing incentives for improving access to and strengthening the capacities of the organized credit system to deliver credit and related services to people living in poverty and vulnerable groups;

d. Expanding financial networks building on existing community networks, promoting attractive opportunities for savings and ensuring equitable access to credit at the local level.

34. Urban poverty should further be addressed by:

a. Promoting and strengthening micro-enterprises, new small businesses, cooperative enterprises, and expanded market and other employment opportunities and, where appropriate, facilitating the transition from the informal to the formal sector;

b. Promoting sustainable livelihoods for people living in urban poverty through the provision or expansion of access to training, education and other employment assistance services, in particular for women, youth, the unemployed and the underemployed;

c. Promoting public and private investments to improve for the deprived the overall human environment and infrastructure, in particular housing, water and sanitation, and public transportation;

d. Ensuring that strategies for shelter give special attention to women and children, bearing in mind the perspectives of women in the development of such strategies;

e. Promoting social and other essential services, including, where necessary, assistance for people to move to areas that offer better employment opportunities, housing, education, health and other social services;

f. Ensuring safety through effective criminal justice administration and protective measures that are responsive to the needs and concerns of the community;

g. Strengthening the role and expanding the means of municipal authorities, non-governmental organizations, universities and other educational institutions, businesses and community organizations, enabling them to be more actively involved in urban planning, policy development and implementation;

h. Ensuring that special measures are taken to protect the displaced, the homeless, street children, unaccompanied minors and children in special and difficult circumstances, orphans, adolescents and single mothers, people with disabilities, and older persons, and to ensure that they are integrated into their communities.

C. Meeting the basic human needs of all

35. Governments, in partnership with all other development actors, in particular with people living in poverty and their organizations, should cooperate to meet the basic human needs of all, including people living in poverty and vulnerable groups, by:

a. Ensuring universal access to basic social services, with particular efforts to facilitate access by people living in poverty and vulnerable groups;

b. Creating public awareness that the satisfaction of basic human needs is an essential element of poverty reduction; these needs are closely interrelated and comprise nutrition, health, water and sanitation, education, employment, housing and participation in cultural and social life;

c. Ensuring full and equal access to social services, especially education, legal services and health-care services for women of all ages and children, recognizing the rights, duties and responsibilities of parents and other persons legally responsible for children, consistent with the Convention on the Rights of the Child;

d. Ensuring that due priority is given and adequate resources made available, at the national, regional and international levels, to combat the threat to individual and public health posed by the rapid spread of HIV/AIDS globally and by the re-emergence of major diseases, such as tuberculosis, malaria, onchocerciasis (river blindness) and diarrhoeal diseases, in particular cholera;

e. Taking particular actions to enhance the productive capacities of indigenous people, ensuring their full and equal access to social services and their participation in the elaboration and implementation of policies that affect their development, with full respect for their cultures, languages, traditions and forms of social organizations, as well as their own initiatives;

f. Providing appropriate social services to enable vulnerable people and people living in poverty to improve their lives, to exercise their rights and to participate fully in all social, economic and political activities and to contribute to social and economic development;

g. Recognizing that improving people's health is inseparably linked to a sound environment;

h. Ensuring physical access to all basic social services for persons who are older, disabled or home-bound;

i. Ensuring that people living in poverty have full and equal access to justice, including knowledge of their rights and, as appropriate, through the provision of free legal assistance. The legal system should be made more sensitive and responsive to the needs and special circumstances of vulnerable and disadvantaged groups in order to ensure a strong and independent administration of justice;

j. Promoting full restorative services, in particular for those who require institutional care or are home-bound, and a comprehensive array of community-based, long-term care services for those facing loss of independence.

36. Governments should implement the commitments that have been made to meet the basic needs of all, with assistance from the international community consistent with chapter 5 of the present Programme of Action, including, *inter alia,* the following:

a. By the year 2000, universal access to basic education and completion of primary education by at least 80 per cent of primary school-age children; closing the gender gap in primary and secondary school education by the year 2005; universal primary education in all countries before the year 2015;

b. By the year 2000, life expectancy of not less than 60 years in any country;

c. By the year 2000, reduction of mortality rates of infants and children under five years of age by one-third of the 1990 level, or 50 to 70 per 1,000 live births, whichever is less; by the year 2015, achievement of an infant mortality rate below 35 per 1,000 live births and an under-five mortality rate below 45 per 1,000;

d. By the year 2000, a reduction in maternal mortality by one half of the 1990 level; by the year 2015, a further reduction by one half;

e. Achieving food security by ensuring a safe and nutritionally adequate food supply, at both the national and international levels, a reasonable degree of stability in the supply of food, as well as physical, social and economic access to enough food for all, while reaffirming that food should not be used as a tool for political pressure;

f. By the year 2000, a reduction of severe and moderate malnutrition among children under five years of age by half of the 1990 level;

g. By the year 2000, attainment by all peoples of the world of a level of health that will permit them to lead a socially and economically productive life, and to this end, ensuring primary health care for all;

h. Making accessible through the primary health-care system reproductive health to all individuals of appropriate ages as soon as possible and no later than the year 2015, in accordance with the Programme of Action of the International Conference on Population and Development, and taking into account the reservations and declarations made at that Conference, especially those concerning the need for parental guidance and parental responsibility;

i. Strengthening efforts and increasing commitments with the aim, by the year 2000, of reducing malaria mortality and morbidity by at least 20 per cent compared to 1995 levels in at least 75 per cent of affected countries, as well as reducing social and economic losses due to malaria in the developing countries, especially in Africa, where the overwhelming majority of both cases and deaths occur;

j. By the year 2000, eradicating, eliminating or controlling major diseases constituting global health problems, in accordance with paragraph 6.12 of Agenda 21;

k. Reducing the adult illiteracy rate—the appropriate age group to be determined in each country—to at least half its 1990 level, with an emphasis on female literacy; achieving universal access to quality education, with particular priority being given to primary and technical education and job training, combating illiteracy, and eliminating gender disparities in access to, retention in and support for education;

l. Providing, on a sustainable basis, access to safe drinking water in sufficient quantities, and proper sanitation for all;

m. Improving the availability of affordable and adequate shelter for all, in accordance with the Global Strategy for Shelter to the Year 2000;

n. Monitoring the implementation of those commitments at the highest appropriate level and considering the possibility of expediting their implementation through the dissemination of sufficient and accurate statistical data and appropriate indicators.

37. Access to social services for people living in poverty and vulnerable groups should be improved through:

a. Facilitating access and improving the quality of education for people living in poverty by establishing schools in unserved areas, providing social services, such as meals and health care, as incentives for families in poverty to keep children in school, and improving the quality of schools in low-income communities;

b. Expanding and improving opportunities for continuing education and training by means of public and private initiatives and non-formal education in order to improve opportunities for people living in poverty, including people with disabilities, and in order to develop the skills and knowledge that they need to better their conditions and livelihoods;

c. Expanding and improving preschool education, both formal and non-formal, including through new learning technologies, radio and television, to overcome some of the disadvantages faced by young children growing up in poverty;

d. Ensuring that people living in poverty and low-income communities have access to quality health care that provides primary health-care services, consistent with the Programme of Action of the International Conference on Population and Development, free of charge or at affordable rates;

e. Promoting cooperation among government agencies, health-care workers, non-governmental organizations, women's organizations and other institutions of civil society in order to develop a comprehensive national strategy for improving reproductive health care and child health-care services and ensuring that people living in poverty have full access to those services, including, *inter alia,* education and services on family planning, safe motherhood and prenatal and postnatal care, and the benefits of breast-feeding, consistent with the Programme of Action of the International Conference on Population and Development;

f. Encouraging health-care workers to work in low-income communities and rural areas, and providing outreach services to make health care available to otherwise unserved areas, recognizing that investing in a primary health-care system that ensures prevention, treatment and rehabilitation for all individuals is an effective means of promoting social and economic development as well as broad participation in society.

D. Enhanced social protection and reduced vulnerability

38. Social protection systems should be based on legislation and, as appropriate, strengthened and expanded, as necessary, in order to protect from poverty people who cannot find work; people who cannot work due to sickness, disability, old age or maternity, or to their caring for children and sick or older relatives; families that have lost a breadwinner through death or marital breakup; and people who have lost their livelihoods due to natural disasters or civil violence, wars or forced displacement. Due attention should be given to people affected by the human immunodeficiency virus/acquired immunodeficiency syndrome (HIV/AIDS) pandemic. Actions to this end should include:

a. Strengthening and expanding programmes targeted to those in need, programmes providing universal basic protection, and social security insurance programmes, with the choice of programmes depending on national financial and administrative capacities;

b. Developing, where necessary, a strategy for a gradual expansion of social protection programmes that provide social security for all, according to a schedule and terms and conditions related to national contexts;

c. Ensuring that social safety nets associated with economic restructuring are considered as complementary strategies to overall poverty reduction and an increase in productive employment. Short term by nature, safety nets must protect people living in poverty and enable them to find productive employment;

d. Designing social protection and support programmes to help people become self-sufficient as fully and quickly as possible, to assist and protect families, to reintegrate people excluded from economic activity and to prevent the social isolation or stigmatization of those who need protection;

e. Exploring a variety of means for raising revenues to strengthen social protection programmes, and promoting efforts by the private sector and voluntary associations to provide social protection and support;

f. Promoting the innovative efforts of self-help organizations, professional associations and other organizations of civil society in this sphere;

g. Expanding and strengthening social protection programmes to protect working people, including the self-employed and their families, from the risk of falling into poverty, by extending coverage to as many as possible, providing benefits quickly and ensuring that entitlements continue when workers change jobs;

h. Ensuring, through appropriate regulation, that contributory social protection plans are efficient and transparent so that the contributions of workers, employers and the State and the accumulation of resources can be monitored by the participants;

i. Ensuring an adequate social safety net under structural adjustment programmes;

j. Ensuring that social protection and social support programmes meet the needs of women, and especially that they take into account women's multiple roles and concerns, in particular the reintegration of women into formal work after periods of absence, support for older women, and the promotion of acceptance of women's multiple roles and responsibilities.

39. Particular efforts should be made to protect children and youth by:

a. Promoting family stability and supporting families in providing mutual support, including in their role as nurturers and educators of children;

b. Promoting social support, including good quality child care and working conditions that allow both parents to reconcile parenthood with working life;

c. Supporting and involving family organizations and networks in community activities;

d. Taking the necessary legislative, administrative, social and educational measures to protect and promote the rights of the child, with particular attention to the girl child;

e. Improving the situation and protecting the rights of children in especially difficult circumstances, including children in areas of armed conflict, children who lack adequate family support, urban street children, abandoned children, children with disabilities, children addicted to narcotic drugs, children affected by war or natural and man-made disasters, unaccompanied minor refugee children, working children, and children who are economically and sexually exploited or abused, including the victims of the sale and trafficking of children; ensuring that they have access to food, shelter, education and health care and are protected from abuse and violence, as well as provided with the necessary social and psychological assistance for their healthy reintegration into society and for family reunification consistent with the Convention on the Rights of the Child; and substituting education for child work;

f. Developing and strengthening programmes targeted at youth living in poverty in order to enhance their economic, educational, social and cultural opportunities, to promote constructive social relations among them and to provide them with connections outside their communities to break the intergenerational cycle of poverty;

g. Addressing the special needs of indigenous children and their families, particularly those living in poor areas, enabling them to benefit adequately from economic and social development programmes, with full respect for their cultures, languages and traditions;

h. Improving the condition of the single parent in society and ensuring that single-parent families and female-headed or female-maintained households receive the social support they need, including support for adequate housing and child care.

40. Particular efforts should be made to protect older persons, including those with disabilities, by:

a. Strengthening family support systems;

b. Improving the situation of older persons, in particular in cases where they lack adequate family support, including rural older persons, working older persons, those affected by armed conflicts and natural or man-made disasters, and those who are exploited, physically or psychologically neglected, or abused;

c. Ensuring that older persons are able to meet their basic human needs through access to social services and social security, that those in need are assisted, and that older persons are protected from abuse and violence and are treated as a resource and not a burden;

d. Providing assistance to grandparents who have been required to assume responsibility for children, particularly of parents who are affected by serious diseases, including AIDS or leprosy, or others who are unable to care for their dependants;

e. Creating a financial environment that encourages people to save for their old age;

f. Strengthening measures and mechanisms to ensure that retired workers do not fall into poverty, taking into account their contribution to the development of their countries;

g. Encouraging and supporting cross-generational participation in policy and programme development and in decision-making bodies at all levels.

41. People and communities should be protected from impoverishment and long-term displacement and exclusion resulting from disasters through the following actions at the national and international levels, as appropriate:

a. Designing effective mechanisms to reduce the impact and to mitigate the effects of natural disasters, such as droughts, earthquakes, cyclones and floods;

b. Developing long-term strategies and contingency plans for the effective mitigation of natural disasters and for famine, including early warning, assessment, information dissemination and management, as well as rapid response strategies, that ensure the quick evolution of relief activities into rehabilitation and development;

c. Developing complementary mechanisms that integrate governmental, intergovernmental and non-governmental efforts, including the establishment of national volunteer corps to support United Nations activities in the areas of humanitarian emergency assistance, as well as mechanisms to promote a smooth transition from relief to rehabilitation, reconstruction and development, in accordance with General Assembly resolutions 46/182 and 49/139 B;

d. Developing and strengthening emergency food reserves as a means to prevent acute food shortages and stabilize prices, with facilities for food storage, transportation and distribution during emergencies, making full use of traditional and market mechanisms;

e. In disaster-prone areas and in cooperation with community-based organizations, developing drought and flood mitigation agronomic practices and resource conservation and infrastructure-building programmes, using food-for-work, where appropriate, and incorporating traditional disaster-response practices that can be rapidly expanded into emergency employment and rebuilding programmes in disaster situations;

f. Establishing the necessary planning and logistical mechanisms to enable quick and effective response in disaster situations to provide food, psychological and social care, medicines, medical supplies and other relief to victims, especially women and children, and ensuring that the relief is effectively targeted to those who need it; and channelling and organizing disaster assistance so as to regenerate the local economy and support resource protection and development efforts;

g. Mobilizing and coordinating regional and international assistance, including assistance from the United Nations system, and from non-governmental organizations, to support the actions of Governments and communities confronting disaster situations;

h. Reducing vulnerability to natural disasters through the development of early warning systems.

Index